2002

Institutionalizing a Broader View of Scholarship Through Boyer's Four Domains

John M. Braxton, William Luckey,
Patricia Helland

ASHE-ERIC Higher Education Report: Volume 29, Number 2
Adrianna J. Kezar, Series Editor

Prepared and published by

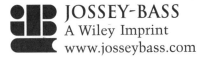 **JOSSEY-BASS**
A Wiley Imprint
www.josseybass.com

In cooperation with

ERIC Clearinghouse on Higher Education
The George Washington University
URL: www.eriche.org

Association for the Study
of Higher Education
URL: www.tiger.coe.missouri.edu/~ashe

Graduate School of Education and Human Development
The George Washington University
URL: www.gwu.edu

Institutionalizing a Broader View of Scholarship Through Boyer's Four Domains
John M. Braxton, William Luckey, Patricia Helland
ASHE-ERIC Higher Education Report: Volume 29, Number 2
Adrianna J. Kezar, Series Editor

This publication was prepared partially with funding from the Office of Educational Research and Improvement, U.S. Department of Education, under contract no. ED-99-00-0036. The opinions expressed in this report do not necessarily reflect the positions or policies of OERI or the Department.

ISSN 0884-0040   electronic ISSN 1536-0709   ISBN 0-7879-5841-7

The **ASHE-ERIC Higher Education Report** is part of the Jossey-Bass Higher and Adult Education Series and is published six times a year by Wiley Subscription Services, Inc., A Wiley Imprint, at Jossey-Bass, 989 Market Street, San Francisco, California 94103-1741.

For subscription information, see the Back Issue/Subscription Order Form in the back of this journal.

CALL FOR PROPOSALS: Prospective authors are strongly encouraged to contact Adrianna Kezar at (301) 405-0868 or kezar@wam.umd.edu.

Visit the Jossey-Bass Web site at **www.josseybass.com.**

Printed in the United States of America on acid-free recycled paper.

Executive Summary

In his influential book *Scholarship Reconsidered: Priorities of the Professoriate,* Ernest Boyer (1990) proposed that the definition of scholarship be broadened beyond the predominant emphasis on the scholarship of discovery to encompass the scholarships of integration, application, and teaching. Boyer's formulations have sparked considerable scholarly attention focused primarily on clarifying the meaning of the domains of scholarship and on criteria and forms of documentation needed to assess scholarship across the four domains (Glassick, Huber, and Maeroff, 1997; Shulman and Hutchings, 1998). This spate of literature and scholarly discussion, coupled with an elapse of over 10 years since the advancement of Boyer's perspective, strongly indicates a need for a stock-taking of this literature. Such a stock-taking requires attention to appraisals of Boyer's arguments by contemporary scholars and various efforts by scholars to clarify the meaning of the domains of scholarship described by Boyer. This volume reviews the major scholarly works on these topics.

Because Boyer's formulations portray how scholarship should be performed rather than how it is performed, an important question emerges: *To what extent do college and university faculty members engage in the work of each of the four domains of scholarship?* Despite the significance of Boyer's arguments, little or no empirical research has addressed this essential question. Response to this fundamental question enables us to gauge the extent to which the four domains of scholarship have become institutionalized into the academic work of college and university faculty members.

The guiding definition of institutionalization used in this volume is: "institutionalization, most broadly conceived, is the process whereby specific cultural elements or cultural objects are adopted by actors in a social system" (Clark, 1971, p. 75). Institutionalization also occurs on three levels: structural, procedural, and incorporation, with incorporation being the highest level (Curry, 1992). We contend that the achievement of all three levels is necessary to sustain the institutionalization of Boyer's four domains of scholarship. Accordingly, we appraise the attainment of these three levels of institutionalization of Boyer's perspective by using data we collected from a national sample of 1,424 faculty members in five types of colleges and universities and four academic disciplines.

We further our understanding of the limitations and possibilities of institutionalization by asking: *What factors impede or facilitate institutionalization of the four domains of scholarship into the scholarly work of college and university faculty members?* In addressing this second overarching question, we discuss factors that facilitate or impede the institutionalization of Boyer's formulations. The factors discussed are state-level instruments of economic development, university-industry research collaboration, the processes used to assess faculty scholarship, faculty workload patterns, the academic reward structure, graduate education, and scholarly role acquisition by community college faculty members.

We also review various approaches to changing the academic reward structure and the process of assessing faculty scholarship, because fundamental changes in these entities are needed to attain the incorporation level of the institutionalization of Boyer's arguments.

Conclusions and Recommendations for Policy and Practice

We advance five conclusions: (1) all four domains of scholarship have attained structural level institutionalization; (2) the scholarships of discovery and teaching have attained procedural level institutionalization, whereas the scholarships of application and integration show progress toward the achievement of this level of institutionalization; (3) the scholarships of discovery and teaching have attained both structural and procedural level

institutionalization; (4) the potential for incorporation level institutionalization of the scholarships of application, integration and teaching exists if
changes supportive of Boyer's formulations transpire in graduate education,
and the academic reward system and its accompanying process of scholarship
assessment; and (5) the scholarship of discovery persists as the most legitimate
and preferred objective of faculty scholarly engagement across the spectrum
of institutions of higher education ranging from liberal arts colleges to research
and doctoral-granting universities.

We also advance a set of eleven recommendations for institutional policy
and practice that are designed to further the institutionalization of Boyer's four
domains of scholarship. Examples of these recommendations are:

- *Assessments of Faculty Scholarship Should Use the Inventory of Scholarship.* We
  also recommend that both publications and unpublished scholarship meeting Shulman and Hutchings's (1998) three criteria of scholarship should
  be used to assess the scholarship of faculty for tenure and promotion decisions. Shulman and Hutchings criteria are discussed in this report.
- *A Definition of the Scholarship of Teaching Must Be Embraced.* The definition we posit is: The purpose of the scholarship of teaching is the development and improvement of pedagogical practices.
- *Institutional Support Mechanisms for Faculty Scholarship Engagement Must
  Be Developed.*
- *Institutional Mission Statements Should Emphasize the Domain of Scholar-
  ship Stressed by the Institution.*
- *Tenure and Promotion Decisions Should Be Based on Performance of the Type
  of Scholarship Stressed by an Institution's Mission Statement.*
- *Graduate School Training Should Foster Scholarship in Each of Boyer's Four
  Domains.*

In addition to such recommendations, this report provides an *Inventory of
Scholarship.* Although Boyer provided some examples of scholarly forms reflective of the objectives of some domains of scholarship, a more concrete specification of forms of scholarship oriented toward each domain is necessary to

measure faculty engagement in each of the four domains of scholarship. The *Inventory of Scholarship* provides such concrete specifications for each of the four domains of scholarship. For each domain, we sort these scholarly forms into three categories: scholarly activities, unpublished scholarly outcomes, and publications. The activities we display under the category of unpublished scholarly outcomes meet the designation of unpublished, publicly observable scholarship if the three criteria of scholarship described by Shulman and Hutchings (1998) are met.

Intended Audience

Provosts, academic deans, chairpersons of academic departments, and individual faculty members will find this volume useful to their efforts to institutionalize Boyer's four domains of scholarship. Scholars who study role performance of the professoriate will also find this monograph to be valuable as it offers another window on faculty research role performance.

The appeal of Boyer's four domains of scholarship resides in the possibility of developing a faculty reward structure that is more congruent with the following: the day-to-day scholarly engagement of most college and university faculty members, the expectations of the lay public for faculty work, and the institutional missions of colleges and universities that do not primarily emphasize scholarship as discovery. This volume provides not only an empirically grounded knowledge and understanding of the extent of faculty engagement in Boyer's four domains of scholarship, but also a knowledge and understanding of the factors that facilitate or impede institutionalization.

References

Boyer, E. L. (1990). *Scholarship reconsidered: Priorities of the professoriate.* Carnegie Foundation for the Advancement of Teaching.

Clark, T. N. (1971). "Institutionalization of innovations in higher education: Four models." In J.V. Baldridge (ed.), *Academic governance: Research on institutional politics and decision-making* (pp. 75–96), Berkeley, CA: McCutchan Publishing.

Curry, B. K. (1992). Instituting enduring innovations: Achieving continuity of change in higher education. ASHE-ERIC Higher Education Report no. 7. Washington, D.C.: George Washington University.

Glassick, C. E., Huber, M. T., and Maeroff, G. I. (1997). *Scholarship assessed: Evaluation of the professoriate.* San Francisco, CA: Jossey-Bass.

Shulman, L. S., and Hutchings, P. (1998). *About the scholarship of teaching and learning.* The Pew scholars national fellowship program. The Carnegie Foundation for the Advancement of Teaching.

Contents

Foreword

Almost every education reform movement in higher education today relates to Ernest Boyer's *Scholarship Reconsidered*. Whether it is service-learning, action research, feminist epistemologies, doctoral education, the engaged campus, or undergraduate research programs, each movement has a connection to Boyer's bold concept of rethinking inquiry and scholarship. He realized that only through a marked rethinking of inquiry could the academy alter its priorities, truly becoming a multipurpose enterprise with attention to teaching, research, and service. His vision for higher education also mirrored the diverse system that has evolved, with institutional missions that differentially emphasize forms of scholarship. Many campuses resonated with this philosophy that was sensitive to mission and complexity. Over the past decade, many campuses have examined their structure, rewards, and culture to identify whether and to what degree changes might be necessary to align their institutions with the type of inquiry appropriate to their mission.

Although hundreds of articles, op ed pieces, and books have been written about *scholarship reconsidered,* there has been no comprehensive study of the institutionalization of Boyer's concept. Braxton, Luckey, and Helland provide this much needed research in this monograph, *Institutionalizing a Broader View of Scholarship Through Boyer's Four Domains.* John M. Braxton, professor of Education at Vanderbilt University, has spent the past several decades studying faculty and scholarship. His insights, drawn from a career of research on these issues, are invaluable. William Luckey, president of Lindsey Wilson College, a campus that has struggled to institutionalize Boyer's concepts, has firsthand experience with these issues. Patricia Helland is a doctoral candidate in higher education administration at Vanderbilt University. Her current research focuses on graduate student education, entering teaching assistants, and norms associated with undergraduate student teaching.

This manuscript has two main audiences: deans, department chairs, and other change agents who are working to align faculty work with institutional mission; and scholars and researchers in higher education who examine faculty work, institutional policy, or change processes. The writing is accessible to both audiences. After an introduction to Boyer's notion of scholarship reconsidered, the authors review the domains of application, discovery, integration, and teaching in separate chapters. Perhaps the most important chapters for practitioners are on factors affecting institutionalization and approaches to altering the academic reward system. These chapters provide context, nuance, and detail for decision makers to consider as they develop policy. Researchers will discover important sections on findings about the individual and organizational factors that affect institutionalization, future research needs, and appendices with details about the research project. Both groups will be interested to find that the scholarships of discovery and teaching have achieved structural and procedural institutionalization. Yet they perhaps will not be surprised that the scholarship of discovery remains the dominant form as the most legitimate and preferred type of scholarship across all institutional types. Recommendations include altering graduate student socialization, the need for college and university presidents and administrators to reinforce institutional missions, the necessity to examine faculty workloads—especially around teaching within certain institutional types—and the importance of clarifying the definition of the scholarship of teaching.

I remain hopeful that a systemic effort that reexamines graduate education, internal and external reward systems, funding, and policy can begin to create a new higher education enterprise that reflects a form of scholarship embedded in our pluralistic system of higher education.

Adrianna J. Kezar
AEHE-ERIC Series Editor

Acknowledgments

We would like to acknowledge the financial support of Lindsey Wilson College and Peabody College, Vanderbilt University, for our research focusing on faculty engagement in the four domains of scholarship delineated by Boyer. Without their support, this research could not have been conducted. We would also like to acknowledge the assistance of Dr. Sylvia Carey and Dr. Wanda Coneal, who helped design and administer the *Faculty Professional Performance Survey.*

Introduction

IN HIS INFLUENTIAL BOOK, *Scholarship Reconsidered: Priorities of the Professoriate,* Boyer (1990) proposes that the definition of scholarship be broadened beyond the predominant emphasis on the scholarship of discovery to encompass the scholarship of integration, the scholarship of application, and the scholarship of teaching. Boyer's formulations have sparked considerable scholarly attention, the bulk of it focusing on clarifying the meaning of the domains of scholarship (e.g., Johnston, 1998; Lynton, 1995; Kreber, 2001b, and Rice, 1991) and on criteria and forms of documentation needed to assess scholarship across the four domains (e.g., Glassick, Huber, and Maeroff, 1997; Shulman and Hutchings, 1998). A search of the Institute for Scientific Information's citation database reveals that more than 160 articles reference Boyer's *Scholarship Reconsidered.* In addition, Boyer's four domains of scholarship have been the primary focus of the Faculty Roles and Rewards Conference held annually by the American Association for Higher Education. This spate of literature and scholarly discussion coupled with an elapse of more than ten years since the advancement of Boyer's perspective strongly indicate a need to take stock of this literature. Such a taking stock requires attention to appraisals of Boyer's arguments by contemporary scholars and various efforts by scholars to clarify the meaning of the domains of scholarship described by Boyer. This volume reviews the major scholarly works on these topics.

Because Boyer's formulations portray how scholarship *should* be performed rather than how it *is* performed, an important question emerges: To what extent do college and university faculty members engage in the work of each of the four domains of scholarship? Despite the significance of Boyer's arguments, little or no empirical research has addressed this essential question. Response to this fundamental question enables us to gauge the extent to which the four domains of scholarship have become institutionalized into the academic work of college and university faculty members. Five specific questions, which we address in this volume, spring from this overarching question. We concentrate on these five questions, using data we collected from a national sample of 1,424 faculty members in five types of colleges and universities and four academic disciplines. Appendix A describes the study in detail. These five questions are as follows:

1. *What is the general level of faculty engagement in each of Boyer's four domains of scholarship? Do faculty levels of engagement in Boyer's four domains of scholarship resemble the general level of publication productivity found in research?* Scholars conclude from their reviews of research that faculty levels of general, career publication productivity are low (Finkelstein, 1984; Creswell, 1985; Fox, 1985). More specifically, Boyer (1990) reports that 41 percent of faculty have never published an article, monograph, or book during their careers. Finkelstein (1984) provides another perspective on this low level of publication performance in Table 5.1 of his book, noting that 43 percent of faculty members had not published during the previous two years. Thus, a similar level of publication activity is demonstrated between the two-year and the career rate of publication performance.

2. *Do faculty levels of engagement in Boyer's four domains of scholarship match Boyer's prescriptions for institutional domain emphasis?* Boyer (1990) urges colleges and universities to define their own mission and develop a faculty reward system that supports the selected mission. Although Boyer contends that some faculty may engage in all four domains of scholarship across the spectrum of colleges and universities, he argues that some domains of scholarship should receive greater emphasis than others in particular types of colleges and universities.

In addressing this question, we make two types of comparisons: between and within institutional type. Comparisons between institutional types entail comparing faculty levels of engagement in the four domains of scholarship across different types of colleges and universities. In contrast, comparisons within institutional types entail comparing faculty level of engagement in each domain of scholarship for each type of college and university represented in our study.

Our study includes faculty who hold appointments at five types of colleges and universities representative of the following categories of the 1994 Carnegie classification of institutions: research I universities, doctoral-granting universities–I, comprehensive universities and colleges–I, liberal arts colleges–I, and liberal arts colleges–II. These types of institutions vary in terms of their institutional missions. At one extreme, liberal arts colleges–II are predominately oriented toward teaching. At the other extreme, research I universities and doctoral-granting universities–I are primarily oriented toward research. Comprehensive universities and colleges–I and liberal arts colleges–I hold a middle ground, as their missions tend to be oriented toward both teaching and research (McGee, 1971; Finnegan, 1993).

3. *Does faculty publication productivity in Boyer's four domains of scholarship across different types of colleges and universities mirror the level of general publication productivity exhibited across different types of colleges and universities?* The mission of colleges and universities exerts a strong influence on the scholarly role performance of academics (Ruscio, 1987). Levels of publication productivity (Blackburn and Lawrence, 1995; Ruscio, 1987; Fox, 1985; Finkelstein, 1984; Fulton and Trow, 1974), work styles, attitudes, beliefs, values, and reference groups of academic professionals vary across different types of colleges and universities (Blackburn and Lawrence, 1995; Ruscio, 1987; Fulton and Trow, 1974). Accordingly, faculty in research and doctoral-granting universities display higher levels of general publication productivity than do their academic counterparts at teaching-oriented colleges and universities (Fulton and Trow, 1974; Finkelstein, 1984; Creswell, 1985; Blackburn and Lawrence, 1995).

4. *Do faculty levels of engagement in Boyer's four domains of scholarship vary across different academic disciplines?* Academic disciplines vary in the level of consensus (high verses low) on such factors as theoretical orientation, appropriate research methods, and the importance of various research questions to the advancement of the discipline (Kuhn, 1962, 1970; Lodahl and Gordon, 1972; Biglan, 1973). Biology and chemistry are

examples of high consensus disciplines, history and sociology of low consensus ones. Braxton and Hargens (1996) conclude from an extensive review of empirical research that faculty in high consensus fields are more oriented toward research than faculty in low consensus fields. In addition, faculty in high consensus fields experience higher rates of publication, lower journal rejection rates, and greater availability of external funding for research than do their low consensus faculty counterparts. In contrast, faculty in low consensus fields are more oriented toward teaching than their faculty colleagues in high consensus disciplines (Braxton and Hargens, 1996). In comparison with high consensus faculty, academics in low consensus disciplines spend more time on teaching and express a greater interest in it. They also tend to receive higher course evaluations and exhibit an affinity for enacting teaching activities and practices designed to improve undergraduate education (Braxton and Hargens, 1996; Braxton, 1995; Braxton, Olsen, and Simmons, 1998). Given such a pattern of differences, the level of faculty engagement in the four domains of scholarship may differ between high consensus (biology and chemistry) and low consensus (history and sociology) academic disciplines. Biology, chemistry, history, and sociology are the four disciplines represented in our study.

5. *Do individual faculty characteristics influence faculty engagement in the four domains of scholarship? Do individual faculty characteristics influence faculty engagement in the four domains of scholarship in the same way that they influence general publication productivity?* Extensive reviews of the literature (Creswell, 1985; Fox, 1985; Creamer, 1998) as well as research by Blackburn and Lawrence (1995) point to one or more of the following individual faculty characteristics as possessing some relationship with general publication productivity: gender, race, professional age, tenure status, and prestige of the doctoral-granting department.

General publication productivity refers to both the form of publication (e.g., article, book, book chapter) and the objective of the scholarship being published (e.g., discovery, application, integration, or teaching). Scholars (e.g., Finkelstein, 1984; Creswell, 1985) conducting reviews of research on publication productivity do not distinguish in their conclusions among different forms of publications, such as book chapters or scholarly books and articles. Moreover, distinctions among publications on the basis of their research objectives (e.g., basic, applied, or integrative) are also not made in the conclusions offered by scholars reviewing the research literature on publication productivity.

We enhance our knowledge and understanding of the limitations and possibilities of institutionalizing Boyer's formulations into the academic work of faculty members at different types of colleges and universities by addressing these five questions through empirical research. We further our understanding of the limitations and possibilities of institutionalization by asking what factors impede or facilitate institutionalization of the four domains of scholarship into the scholarly work of college and university faculty members. We also pursue this question in this volume. In addressing this second overarching question, we discuss factors that facilitate or impede the institutionalization of Boyer's formulations.

The guiding definition of institutionalization used in this volume is "institutionalization, most broadly conceived, is the process whereby specific cultural elements or cultural objects are adopted by actors in a social system" (Clark, 1971, p. 75). Similar to Clark's definition, Berman and McLaughlin (1974) define institutionalization as the point at which an innovative practice loses its "special project" status and becomes part of the routine behavior of the system.

Levels of Institutionalization

Institutionalization also occurs on three levels: structural, procedural, and incorporation (Curry, 1991). We contend that the achievement of all three levels is necessary to sustain the institutionalization of Boyer's four domains of scholarship. Accordingly, this volume appraises the attainment of each level of institutionalization of Boyer's perspective.

Structural

At the structural level, a change is represented in several ways throughout the institution. There is a basic knowledge of the behaviors associated with the innovation, and those involved understand how to perform the behaviors. There is also some form of measurement in place for assessing how individuals perform each behavior (Goodman and Associates, 1982). In addition to new or changed behaviors, it is also possible that the organizational structure will have changed to accommodate additional personnel to administer the new program.

By addressing the first question guiding this monograph, the findings of our study enable us to gauge the extent of structural institutionalization of Boyer's four domains of scholarship. Specifically, we use general levels of faculty engagement as an index of the extent of structural level institutionalization of each of the four domains of scholarship. We measure general levels of faculty engagement using both unpublished and published scholarly outcomes. We discuss the use of these two measures in the section titled "Assessment of Faculty Scholarship in Boyer's Four Domains" in the next chapter.

Procedural

At the procedural level, behaviors and policies associated with the innovation become standard. In essence, they become part of the standard operating procedure of the disciplinary department or the entire institution. As for individuals in the organization, this level shows their preferences for the behaviors identified at the structural level.

By addressing this volume's second guiding question, we gauge the extent of procedural level institutionalization of Boyer's perspective. Because the attainment of procedural level institutionalization occurs when the behaviors and policies associated with the object of institutionalization become standard operating procedure of a college or university (Curry, 1991), we use the extent to which faculty engage in the domain of scholarship prescribed for their type of college or university by Boyer as an indicator of procedural level institutionalization. If faculty members follow Boyer's prescriptions for the type of scholarship that Boyer prescribes for their type of college or university, then we can assume that such scholarly efforts have become standard operating procedure. We use unpublished scholarly outcomes and publications as indicators of domain scholarship engagement.

Incorporation

The most in-depth level of institutionalization is incorporation, where the values and norms associated with the innovation are incorporated into an organization's culture. With this normative consensus comes an awareness of how others are performing the behavior as well as an agreement on the appropriateness of the behavior. The values themselves are based on a social consensus relevant to specific behaviors (Goodman and Associates, 1982). Deal and Kennedy (1982) discuss the idea that employees identify and act on the values of their organizations. Therefore, unless an innovation becomes valued, or institutionalized, it will not have anyone to lobby for its continuation. If no one in the organization acts on that value, the innovation will fail. Of course, throughout the life of an innovation before it becomes institutionalized, it may go through changes of its own before the final outcome. Those differences, from idea to implementation to institutionalization, may be minor or more dramatic in nature.

"Factors Affecting the Institutionalization of a Broader Definition of Scholarship" discusses the extent of incorporation level institutionalization of Boyer's perspective by noting forces that foster or impede the attainment of this level of institutionalization. In particular, it assesses the graduate school socialization process and the values individual faculty members, departmental colleagues, and the institution hold toward the scholarships of application, discovery, integration, and teaching.

Overview of the Volume

In addition to this introduction, eight chapters are included in the volume. The chapter titled "The Four Domains of Scholarship: Toward a Rethinking of Scholarly Role Performance" reviews Boyer's arguments for expanding the parameters of scholarship beyond discovery to encompass the scholarship of application, the scholarship of integration, and the scholarship of teaching. It also presents perspectives on scholarship that predate Boyer's formulations as well as contemporary assessments of Boyer. Contemporary assessments of Boyer include a presentation of different scholarly forms judged legitimate indices of scholarship.

The next four chapters—"The Scholarship of Application," "The Scholarship of Discovery," "The Scholarship of Integration," and "The Scholarship of Teaching"—are devoted to the four domains. Each chapter presents various perspectives on the scholarly objectives of the focal domain of scholarship found in the literature. The chapters also address each of the five questions listed earlier in this chapter, using findings from our faculty professional performance study (Appendix A).

The chapter following, "Factors Affecting the Institutionalization of a Broader Definition of Scholarship," concentrates on presenting various levels of institutionalization. It also describes factors that impede or facilitate one or more levels of institutionalization of Boyer's perspective. The factors described are the academic reward structure, graduate education, role acquisition, scholarly values, assessment of faculty scholarship, state level economic development, faculty workload, and university-industry research collaboration.

The following chapter presents approaches for changing the academic reward structure to align with institutional missions. It also provides ways in which the process of assessing faculty scholarship performance can be changed to better embrace Boyer's formulations.

The final chapter summarizes findings of our study, organized by each of the five research questions. It also presents five conclusions derived from our findings and literature reviewed in this volume, eleven recommendations designed to enhance the institutionalization of Boyer's perspectives, and recommendations for further study.

Appendix A summarizes the research methods and statistical procedures used in conducting our study and contains the statistical tables supporting findings of our study. Appendix B, "The Inventory of Scholarship," includes the various forms of scholarship subsumed under Boyer's four domains.

Intended Audience

Provosts, academic deans, chairs of academic departments, members of tenure and promotion committees, officers and pertinent committee members of professional and scholarly associations, and individual faculty members will find this volume useful in their efforts to institutionalize Boyer's four domains of scholarship. Scholars who study the professoriate's role performance will also find this monograph to be of value, as it offers another window on faculty research role performance.

The appeal of Boyer's four domains of scholarship resides in the possibility of developing a faculty reward structure that is more congruent with the day-to-day scholarly engagement of most college and university faculty members, the expectations of the lay public for faculty work, and the institutional missions of colleges and universities that do not primarily emphasize scholarship as discovery. This volume provides not only an empirically grounded knowledge and understanding of the extent of faculty engagement in Boyer's four domains of scholarship but also the knowledge and understanding of the factors that facilitate or impede institutionalization.

The Four Domains of Scholarship: Toward a Rethinking of Scholarly Role Performance

BOYER'S CALL TO BROADEN the meaning of scholarship beyond discovery to include application, integration, and teaching springs from issues external and internal to higher education. Several basic external issues confront higher education, indicating a need for a broader definition of scholarship.

First, colleges and universities need to serve society (Boyer, 1990). Growing social and political problems require expert advice (Glassick, Huber, and Maeroff, 1997). These social and political problems include underperforming public schools, pollution, urban decay, and neglected children, while global problems include acid rain, AIDS, and the supply of energy (Boyer, 1990). These consequential problems require that college and university faculty apply their disciplinary knowledge and skill to address these nearly intractable problems. Handlin (1986) puts the need for scholarly engagement in the problems of society into sharp focus, contending that scholarship proves its worth through service to the nation and the world. Society expects higher education to be of service (Glassick, Huber, and Maeroff, 1997).

The second issue centers on public expectations for undergraduate teaching. The public holds that undergraduate instruction is the most important activity of college and university faculty members (Ewell, 1994). The lay public also expects faculty to spend more time on teaching undergraduates than on research and scholarship (Volkwein and Carbone, 1994). Boyer (1990) asserts, however, that research activity competes with teaching for valuable faculty time. Instruction loses out as faculty teaching loads are reduced and teaching assistants rather than faculty instruct large undergraduate college classes

(Boyer, 1990). Consequently, the expectations of parents, legislators, students, and trustees for faculty commitment to undergraduate college teaching go unmet. To serve students and assuage public expectations, a broader definition of scholarship beyond discovery is needed (Boyer, 1990).

The need for a broader definition of scholarship also springs from the special commitment of colleges and universities to prepare an educated citizenry (Rice, 1992). Increasingly more diverse populations need the intellectual preparation necessary for such a role, so that a genuine democracy arises from such preparation (Rice, 1992). A broader conception of scholarship is needed to realize this commitment (Rice, 1992).

Faculty academic work and the prevailing faculty reward structure constitute the primary internal issues giving rise to Boyer's call for an expanded definition of scholarship. Boyer (1990) argues that the current faculty reward structure fails to reflect the range of professional activities that faculty perform (p. 16), as this structure counts research, or the scholarship of discovery, as the most legitimate and preferred type of scholarship (p. 2). Moreover, the prevailing reward structure uses publications to appraise the productivity of the scholar as researcher. Boyer asserts that such a narrow view of scholarship and its measurement adversely affects the morale of the professoriate, the vitality of individual colleges and universities, and the welfare of students (p. 2).

Boyer does not, however, denigrate this dominant view of scholarship for the research university, as he holds that it is appropriate for some institutions that embrace research as their institutional mission (p. 12). He does assert that this commanding view is inappropriate for other types of colleges and universities. Put differently, the dominant model of a scholar and his/her productivity fails to align with the mission of most colleges and universities. Accordingly, Boyer presents prescriptions for individual faculty domain performance by institutional type: research universities, doctoral-granting universities, comprehensive universities and colleges, liberal arts colleges, and community colleges. His prescriptions align with

> **The dominant model of a scholar and his/her productivity fails to align with the mission of most colleges and universities.**

the institutional missions of this range of different types of colleges and universities. We describe Boyer's prescriptions for institutional domain emphasis for each of the domains of scholarship in the chapters of this volume focusing on each domain.

Given these formulations, Boyer argues for the expansion of the definition of scholarship beyond discovery to include the scholarship of application, integration, and teaching. Boyer is clear, however, that his call for the expansion of the definition of scholarship is *not* a call for greater balance between teaching and research in the faculty reward structure (1990, p. 16). Rather, his argument calls for ascribing scholarly legitimacy to the full range of academic work—work defined by application, discovery, integration, and teaching. We present Boyer's formulations for the objectives of each of these four domains in corresponding chapters of this volume.

Boyer also advances four "mandates" that should apply to all faculty members (p. 27). These mandates constitute essential conditions for expanding the boundaries of the definition of scholarship. The first of these essential conditions stipulates that all faculty should exhibit the ability to conduct original research and present it to peers for their review. Boyer points to the doctoral dissertation as an example.

A second mandate ordains that all academic professionals should keep up with advancements in their academic fields and remain professionally engaged. Such activity should occur across the span of one's academic career. Boyer states that this mandate may be accomplished in a variety of ways. Some academics may demonstrate this activity through new research and publications. Boyer holds that not all faculty members need to demonstrate their active engagement in this manner. He suggests that active professional engagement also entails reading the literature to keep up with advancements in one's academic discipline. To demonstrate such activity, Boyer suggests that faculty write a paper that identifies important new developments in their field and justify their choices. Such a paper could be reviewed by peers (p. 28).

Boyer's third mandate centers on the propriety of faculty work. He holds that the highest standards of integrity in teaching and research should characterize the work of faculty members.

The fourth mandate is that all academic work of faculty members must be painstakingly appraised. Such assessment should apply regardless of the form the scholarship takes. Boyer asserts that effective approaches to assessing work in all four domains of scholarship must be developed. Moreover, he clearly takes the position that the primary standard of tenure and promotion should not continue to be research (discovery) and publication (1990, p. 34).

To bolster this essential condition, Boyer argues for the development of flexible approaches to assessing faculty scholarship that go beyond the scholarship of discovery and publications in the form of refereed journal articles and scholarly books (p. 35). He asserts a need for the use of a broader range of writings. For example, he suggests textbooks and "popular writing" for laypersons or nonspecialists as such forms of writing. He also states that such writing should be reviewed by peers. In addition to such writing forms, Boyer cites computer software, television, and videocassettes as acceptable ways to communicate scholarship (p. 36). Boyer also calls for the use of written documentation for use in the assessment of faculty scholarship. Such written documentation should accompany the various forms of scholarship presented for assessment. Boyer suggests the use of portfolios for such documentation (p. 40).

In summary, the thrust of Boyer's call to expand the definition of scholarship entails two aspects. First, he argues for the legitimization of scholarship other than discovery to include application, integration, and teaching. Put differently, scholarship should have objectives other than the discovery of new knowledge. We provide extensive discussions of the objectives of the scholarship of application, integration, teaching, and discovery in subsequent chapters of this volume. Second, Boyer calls for flexibility in the assessment of faculty scholarly performance, arguing for the use of scholarly forms apart from articles in refereed journals and scholarly books. His assertions stem from the incongruity between the faculty reward structure and the full range of academic work performed by faculty. Such incongruence undermines the mission of colleges and universities not oriented toward research. As we learn from the next section of this chapter, scholars predating Boyer also made similar arguments about the meaning of scholarship and its appraisal.

Perspectives on Scholarship Before Boyer

Scholars predating Boyer address both the aims of scholarship and the need to assess scholarship using forms other than articles published in refereed journals and scholarly books. Miller (1972) and Seldin (1980), for example, both expand the definition of scholarship by making distinctions between basic and applied research. *Basic research* and *the scholarship of discovery* are interchangeable terms, whereas *applied research* represents a facet of Boyer's and other scholars' view of the scholarship of application. Miller states that institutional and departmental priorities should govern the emphasis placed on either in the faculty evaluation process (p. 68). Seldin also acknowledges a distinction between basic and applied research, maintaining that institutions must make clear their preferences for these two types of scholarship (p. 134).

Although expansion of the measurement of scholarly role performance beyond refereed journal articles and scholarly books is their primary intent, Braxton and Toombs (1982) and Pellino, Blackburn, and Boberg (1984) also implicitly enlarge the boundaries of scholarship. In addition to scholarship as research and publication, Pellino, Blackburn, and Boberg empirically identify five other dimensions of scholarship. Two dimensions parallel two of Boyer's domains of scholarship (application and teaching): "scholarship as community service" and "scholarship as pedagogy." These dimensions are derived from faculty perceptions of the extent to which the items making up these dimensions are characteristic of their role as a scholar.

Braxton and Toombs (1982) also empirically delineate some categories of scholarly activities apart from the scholarship of discovery, including institutional-departmental activities, public service activities, and course content and activities. These categories also parallel Boyer's domains of application and teaching. They were identified by a panel of ten experts on research and graduate education, who assessed the extent to which doctoral research training is used in the performance of the activities making up these three categories.

Scholars predating Boyer also recommend more flexible criteria for tenure and promotion decisions. Miller (1972, 1987) recommends that nonrefereed publications also receive consideration and suggests the use of special reports written for the college or other groups. Seldin (1980) also opposes the sole use of refereed journal articles in tenure and promotion decisions. In addition, Braxton and Bayer (1986) advocated the use of written, unpublished reports of funded research and computer software programs as additional indices of scholarly performance.

Earlier efforts (Braxton and Toombs, 1982; Pellino, Blackburn, and Boberg, 1984) to expand the boundaries of scholarship were also developed because of the infrequency of faculty publication productivity noted by Ladd (1979): "an ascendant model in academe, positing what faculty should be doing, is seriously out of touch with what they actually do and want to do." Ladd, like Boyer, also finds the dominant model of faculty scholarship problematic, especially the primary reliance on published articles in the faculty reward structure. A need for forms of scholarship that reflect the day-to-day scholarly activities of faculty members underlies Ladd's perspective. This view finds reinforcement in Blackburn's assertion (1974) that 90 percent of faculty who seldom or never publish are neither unscholarly nor unproductive.

The work of Braxton and Toombs (1982) and Pellino, Blackburn, and Boberg (1984) seeks to empirically delineate scholarly activities distinct from scholarly books and refereed journal articles that reflect the day-to-day scholarly activities of faculty members. Braxton and Toombs identify 71 scholarly activities distinct from publications in the form of refereed journal articles, scholarly books, and monographs. These activities take the form of outcomes of scholarship as well as scholarship as a process.

Braxton and Toombs classify these activities into two domains, one focusing on the academic discipline and disciplinary colleagues (External Disciplinary-Colleague Domain), the other on activities done for the institution or local community (Institutional Local-Community Domain). Extramural lectures, ancillary disciplinary writings (e.g., critical book reviews and edited books), disciplinary readings (reading of books and articles to keep up with advancements in knowledge), informal communications with colleagues (letters and telephone conversations), and disciplinary association activities (e.g., presenting a paper and serving as chair of a meeting session) constitute subdimensions of the External Disciplinary-Colleague Domain. Subdimensions of the Institutional Local-Community Domain are public talks and lectures on current disciplinary topics (e.g., a talk on a local radio station or a talk for a local women's organization), institutional-departmental activities (e.g., conducting a study to help solve a departmental problem and assisting in institutional preparation for accreditation review), course content and activities (e.g., a lecture on topics from current journal articles not covered in course readings), public service activities (e.g., seminars conducted for laypersons on current disciplinary topics and studies conducted for local governmental agencies), and public disciplinary writings (e.g., articles on current disciplinary topics published in a local newspaper and textbooks published).

Dimensions of faculty scholarship delineated by Pellino, Blackburn, and Boberg (1984) also contain scholarly forms apart from refereed journal articles and scholarly books. Some of these forms subsumed under the dimension "scholarship as professional activity" are reviewing proposals for a funding agency, serving as a member on an accreditation team, delivering a colloquium open to faculty and students, serving on an editorial board of a journal, and reviewing articles for a professional journal. "Scholarship as an artistic endeavor" also contains scholarly forms such as performing or exhibiting an artistic work, practicing a skill, and engaging in writing (poetry, essays). Examples of scholarly forms included in the dimension "scholarship as engagement with the novel" are developing a new process for dealing with a problem and introducing some result of one's scholarship in a consultation. Engaging in off-campus consulting and delivering a talk to a local civic or religious organization are forms reflective of "scholarship as community service." The dimension "scholarship as pedagogy" contains nine scholarly activities apart from refereed journal articles and scholarly books. Noteworthy examples are constructing a novel examination/testing practice, playing a major role in a unit's or college's curriculum revision, making a presentation to colleagues about new instructional techniques, and developing a new set of lectures.

Like those of Braxton and Toombs (1982), many of the scholarly forms identified by Pellino, Blackburn, and Boberg (1984) reflect scholarship as process as well as an observable outcome or product. This differentiation between scholarship as process and as product paves the way for another important distinction: the distinction between scholarly activities and scholarship. Scholarship denotes an outcome or product observable by others, whereas scholarly activities denote a process that applies professional knowledge and skill. This distinction manifests itself in contemporary perspectives on Boyer's arguments. We discuss these contemporary perspectives in the next section of this chapter.

Scholars predating Boyer's *Scholarship Reconsidered* bolster his call to expand the boundaries of scholarship and the forms of scholarship used in the faculty appraisal process. Their scholarship fills important gaps in Boyer's work. To elaborate, Boyer fails to recognize the importance of low faculty publication productivity in his argument concentrating on the need for a faculty reward structure that matches the full range of faculty academic work. The need to acknowledge the day-to-day scholarly activities of faculty members who seldom or never publish greatly bolsters Boyer's argument for not only the expansion of the boundaries of scholarship but also the use of scholarly forms other than refereed journal articles and scholarly books in faculty assessment.

Although Boyer offers a few suggestions for alternative scholarly forms for the assessment of faculty, these suggestions are of limited use in the development of fine-grained approaches to assess faculty performance in the four domains of scholarship. Glassick, Huber, and Maeroff (1997) echo this criticism in their efforts to offer approaches to faculty assessment using Boyer's four domains of scholarship. We offer a broad overview of these approaches in the next section of this chapter and more detailed review in a subsequent chapter of this volume. Nevertheless, scholars predating Boyer provide numerous examples of scholarly forms that reflect the scholarship of application, integration, and teaching. These forms identified by Braxton and Toombs (1982) and Pellino, Blackburn, and Boberg (1984) provide the basis for the delineation of scholarly forms that reflect the various domains of scholarship. We present these scholarly forms in Appendix B. The research of Braxton and Toombs (1982) and Pellino, Blackburn, and Boberg (1984) also serves as a foundation for our research study described in Appendix A.

Contemporary Perspectives on Boyer: Concurrence and Criticism

Boyer's *Scholarship Reconsidered* is one of the most frequently cited publications in the last decade. A search of the Social Science Citation Index yielded 168 citations as of May 2000. The vast majority of these citations, however, are simply cursory mentions of the book. This section presents contemporary assessments of Boyer's formulations. Compelling ideas and perspectives give rise to supportive and critical scholarship. Boyer's formulations are no exception. The contemporary perspectives advanced by scholars refine and extend Boyer's formulations.

Two important books on the assessment of faculty work acknowledge the significance of Boyer's call to expand the boundaries of scholarship: Centra's *Reflective Faculty Evaluation* (1993) and Braskamp and Ory's *Assessing Faculty Work* (1994). Centra devotes several pages of his volume to descriptions of the four domains of scholarship described by Boyer. He concurs with Boyer's arguments for expanding the definition of scholarship by noting that institutional missions and institutional responsibilities receive recognition through such an expansion. Centra also asserts that by labeling integrative research, teaching, and service as scholarship, such professional activities may receive recognition by the academic community, acceptance currently overshadowed by the prestige of the scholarship of discovery. Moreover, individual faculty members who perform them will also receive the credit due.

Like Centra, Braskamp and Ory (1994) view Boyer's call to expand the parameters of scholarship as important to achieving the mission and responsibilities of individual colleges and universities. They assert that the achievement of the mission and responsibilities of individual colleges and universities depends on an acknowledgment of the complexity of academic work. The domains of scholarship described by Boyer encompass such complexity.

Although the four domains of scholarship constitute a taxonomy of scholarship, Paulsen and Feldman (1995) and Rice (1992) offer analytical schema to view these four domains of scholarship. Both schemes speak to the functions played by the four domains of scholarship. Paulsen and Feldman view them as functional elements in the scholarship action system, whereas Rice views them as representing polarities of two dimensions of knowing.

Each domain of scholarship advanced by Boyer is important to the maintenance and effectiveness of scholarship as an activity in colleges and universities.

Each domain of scholarship advanced by Boyer is important to the maintenance and effectiveness of scholarship as an activity in colleges and universities. Paulsen and Feldman (1995) apply Talcott Parsons's four functional imperatives for social action systems to the case of scholarship in colleges and universities. Paulsen and Feldman view scholarship as a social action system. To elaborate, they view faculty activities that use specialized knowledge or expertise in their performance as characterizing the scholarship action system. Viewing scholarship as a social action system is important, because it demonstrates the dependency of scholarship on support from the environment external to colleges and universities or the lay public. Such a demonstration offers a compelling rationale for the institutionalization of Boyer's four domains of scholarship, given the external issues that have given rise to his formulations.

Parsons and Smelser (1956) posit that human action in any social system depends on the adequate performance of four independent functional imperatives: adaptation, goal attainment, pattern maintenance, and integration. These functions are organized around subsystems of a given social action system. Each of the four functions must be adequately performed for a social action system to continue to exist and be effective. These four functions may also be classified as internal or external in their orientation. An external orientation focuses on the interactions between the social system and the external environment (Parsons and Platt, 1973). Adaptation and goal attainment possess an external orientation, whereas pattern maintenance and integration hold an internal orientation (Parsons and Platt, 1973). Like other social systems, scholarship must contribute to society and receive support from it.

Paulsen and Feldman (1995) assert that three of the four subsystems of the scholarship action system they delineate correspond to one of Boyer's domains of scholarship. The three subsystems relevant to Boyer are pattern maintenance (the scholarship of research and graduate teaching), adaptation (the scholarship of teaching), and goal attainment (the scholarship of service). More specifically, the scholarship of research and graduate teaching matches

Boyer's scholarship of discovery, the scholarship of teaching corresponds to Boyer's scholarship of teaching, and the scholarship of service coincides with Boyer's scholarship of application. Paulsen and Feldman assert, however, that the functional imperative of integration does not match Boyer's scholarship of integration. They argue that Boyer's scholarship of integration occurs across these three matching functional subsystems of the scholarship action system. They also assert that in terms of the four functional imperatives, integrated knowledge produced through the scholarship of integration does not perform the function of integration in the scholarship social action system needed for this social system to be effective and maintained.

Paulsen and Feldman contend that their analytical model demonstrates the necessity of each function performed by the dimensions of scholarship they have delineated as making up the scholarship action system. Although Paulsen and Feldman (1995) fail to assign a distinct functional role to the scholarship of integration, the stress they place on the indispensability of the various dimensions of scholarship resonates quite well with the external impetus to Boyer's call to broaden the parameters of what constitutes faculty scholarship. Paulsen and Feldman's assignment of the scholarships of application (goal attainment) and teaching (adaptation) to functions with an orientation toward making contributions to society underscores the importance of these two domains of scholarship to meeting the expectations of society for scholarship that serves the teaching of undergraduates and helps alleviate social and political problems, two external issues confronting higher education that gave rise to Boyer's formulations. Consequently, the theoretical model advanced by Paulsen and Feldman provides a cogent rationale for use by institutional policymakers striving for the institutionalization of Boyer's four domains of scholarship. We offer a more detailed discussion of the relationship of Boyer's domains of scholarship to Paulsen and Feldman's application of Parson's four functional imperatives to the scholarship action system in subsequent chapters of this volume.

According to Rice (1992), Boyer's domains of scholarship also allocate recognition to different ways of knowing represented among college and university faculty members. Rice identifies two basic polarities—concrete-abstract and reflective-active—to array ways of knowing. The concrete-abstract polarity concerns how knowledge is perceived, with the abstract pole centering on objective, value-free knowledge derived from an analytical approach and knowledge acquired through concrete experiences and relationships defining the concrete end of the continuum. Values point to worthwhile knowledge. How learning is processed is portrayed by the reflective-active continuum, stressing instrumental and practical knowledge. The reflective end of the continuum focuses on the acquisition of knowledge for its own sake, whereas the active end of the continuum stresses the knowledge acquired through active engagement with the world.

Rice arrays Boyer's four domains of scholarship according to these dimensions and their polarities. He classifies the scholarship of discovery as abstract and reflective, the scholarship of application as abstract and active, the scholarship of integration as concrete and reflective, and the scholarship of teaching as concrete and active. Thus, the four domains of scholarship match the learning styles of faculty.

Davis and Chandler (1998) and Schön (1995) offer critical appraisals of Boyer. Although Davis and Chandler support Boyer's objectives, they contend that the academic reward structure represents a barrier to the kind of changes Boyer recommends. They assert that faculty rewards are allocated by boards of trustees and administrators and that faculty decision making on academic matters yields little impact. Davis and Chandler posit that the organization structure and its corresponding reward structure must change. We discuss further the academic reward structure as well as other forces that facilitate or impede the institutionalization of Boyer's arguments in the chapter titled "Factors Affecting the Institutionalization of a Broader Definition of Scholarship."

Schön (1995) also supports Boyer's call to expand to the parameters of scholarship. He asserts, however, that the scholarships of application, integration, and teaching rest on a different epistemology base than does the scholarship of discovery. Schön posits that the scholarship of discovery emanates from research characterized by technical rationality, whereas the scholarships of application, integration, and teaching spring from action research. He states that technical rationality is professional knowledge derived from systematic knowledge. Practice with such knowledge entails the adjustment of technical means to ends that are clear, fixed, and internally consistent.

Schön (1995) contends, however, that epistemology useful to practice stems from the type of knowledge that practitioners exhibit in situations characterized as unique, uncertain, and complex. Such knowledge manifests itself in action or in day-to-day professional activities. This form of knowledge, which serves the scholarships of application, integration, and teaching, springs from a process entailing first the delineation of a problematic situation and then the development of strategies for possible solutions to the problem. These strategies are in turn applied to new situations similar to the initial situation. Put differently, these strategies or this practice knowledge comes from a process of reflection on one's action and then from a reflection on this reflection-in-action. Such newly created knowledge derived from practice can be used in future opportunities for approaching problematic situations. Schön labels such an epistemology *action research*.

Like Boyer (1990), Schön holds that new knowledge may result from engagement in the scholarship of application. He posits that new knowledge emerges from action research as he describes it.

Schön (1995) asserts that acceptance of the scholarships of application, integration, and teaching as accepted forms of scholarship in colleges and universities hinges on acceptance of action research as a legitimate approach to generating knowledge. He holds that the legitimacy of action research depends on the development of faculty peers capable of assessing and facilitating its development.

Assessment of Faculty Scholarship in Boyer's Four Domains

Contemporary appraisals of Boyer's formulations also concentrate on the assessment of faculty performance in the four domains of scholarship described by Boyer. This chapter offers a broad overview of these perspectives, with these and other perspectives described more fully in "Approaches to Altering the Academic Reward System."

Nettlesome issues arise from Boyer's view that publications in refereed journals and scholarly books should not be the primary criteria used to assess faculty performance in each of the four domains of scholarship he describes. As indicated earlier, Boyer contends that other writings or documented evidence of scholarship may be used for faculty assessment. Although Boyer offers a few examples of such forms, these examples provide an insufficient foundation for assessing faculty scholarship performance.

In *Scholarship Assessed: Evaluation of the Professoriate* (1997), Glassick, Huber, and Maeroff capture such concerns: "the ink was barely dry when we started to get calls and letters that said, in effect, It's one thing to give scholarship a larger meaning, but the real issue revolves around how to assess other forms of scholarship" (p. 21). Toward a resolution of this issue, Glassick, Huber, and Maeroff describe six criteria to assess forms of scholarship apart from articles in refereed journals and scholarly books: clear goals, adequate preparation, appropriate methods, significant results, effective presentation, and reflective critique. Glassick, Huber, and Maeroff posit that these six criteria can be applied across the four domains of scholarship. They assert that these six criteria provide a framework for assessing faculty scholarship. Accordingly, these six criteria may be used to appraise a variety of scholarly forms, including publications. Each criterion is described more fully in "Approaches to Altering the Academic Reward System."

The perspectives emanating from Boyer's mandate that scholarly forms apart from scholarly books and articles in refereed journals be used in assessing faculty scholarship process may be arrayed on a continuum. At one extreme, publications of some form are viewed as legitimate forms of scholarship. Richlin (2001) provides the extreme view at this end of the continuum. To elaborate, she argues that publication in formal, peer-reviewed journals constitutes scholarship distinct from scholarship as a process. In making this argument, Richlin writes about the distinction between scholarly teaching and the scholarship of teaching. Nevertheless, her perspective may be applied to the other domains of scholarship. Clearly, Richlin's view resonates with what Braxton and Del Favero (forthcoming) label the traditional faculty scholarship assessment template. Scholarly books, book chapters, refereed journal articles, and citations to published works constitute core elements of this template. Richlin's extreme position may be relaxed somewhat if publications in a variety of forms are viewed as an appropriate form of scholarship. Examples of such publications include textbooks and writings for the popular press.

Scholarly activities may be placed at the opposite end of this continuum. Using faculty perceptions of what faculty scholarship is, Sundre (1992) identifies faculty activities as attributes of faculty scholarship. Sundre's findings concur with the view of Braxton and Toombs (1982) and Pellino, Blackburn, and Boberg (1984) that scholarship is a process as well as a product. Scholarly activities involve the application of disciplinary knowledge and skill in their performance (Braxton and Bayer, 1986). Based on this perspective, many of the day-to-day activities of academics emerge as forms of scholarship if such activities apply disciplinary knowledge and skill in their performance. An inventory of such scholarly activities is exhibited in Appendix B.

Unpublished but publicly observable outcomes of scholarly activity occupy middle ground on this continuum. Shulman and Hutchings (1998) delineate three necessary characteristics for a scholarly form to be labeled scholarship: it must be public, amenable to critical appraisal, and in a form that permits exchange and use by other members of the scholarly community. Unpublished but publicly observable outcomes of scholarly activity possess these three essential characteristics. Braxton and Del Favero (forthcoming) point to papers, presentations, reports, videos, computer software, and Web sites as publicly observable but unpublished forms of scholarship. Moreover, presentations must be recorded (audiotaped or videotaped) in some way so that individuals not in attendance may listen to or view the presentation. A more extensive list of such forms of scholarship is included in Appendix B. Some scholarly forms meeting the six criteria described by Glassick, Huber, and Maeroff (1997) may also be labeled *scholarship*. This view also occupies a middling position with publicly observable but unpublished scholarship on the continuum of forms suitable for use in the assessment of faculty scholarship performance in the academic reward system.

The introduction to this volume lists a set of questions pursued in this volume. We address some of these questions using data we collected. In attending to those questions that pertain to faculty engagement in the four domains of scholarship, we use measures of such engagement that correspond to the three forms of scholarship arrayed on the continuum presented above: scholarly activities, unpublished scholarly outcomes, and publications. But we concur with the three criteria posited by Shulman and Hutchings (1998) and demarcate as scholarship unpublished scholarly outcomes and publications. We use unpublished scholarly outcomes as a proxy measure of unpublished, publicly observable scholarship. Our unpublished scholarly outcomes need only a publicly observable form to meet Shulman and Hutchings's criteria for scholarship (1998). The application of these three criteria to unpublished scholarly outcomes resonates with Boyer's call for indicators of scholarship other than publications. As stated in the introduction, unpublished scholarly outcomes and publications provide indicators of scholarship engagement that enable us to assess the extent of structural and procedural level institutionalization of Boyer's perspective.

The next four chapters of this volume concentrate on the four domains of scholarship Boyer describes. Each chapter describes perspectives on the scholarly objectives of the focal scholarly domain found in the literature and presents findings from our study that address the questions advanced in the introduction to this volume.

The Scholarship of Application

PROFESSIONAL ACTIVITIES of college professors may vary from college to college and university to university, but it is a basic principle that the priorities of the professoriate remain teaching, research, and service. Although service is always mentioned, it is rarely a driving force behind achieving tenure or promotion to full professor. The scholarship of application addresses service and attempts to bring it to the forefront of scholarly activities, particularly to give it the same credence as teaching and research.

The scholarship of application is the application of disciplinary knowledge and skill to help address important societal and institutional problems. Boyer (1990) contends that through practice and through the application of disciplinary knowledge, new theoretical understanding and knowledge can be derived. Although the purpose of any of the four domains is to generate new knowledge and disseminate it to others in various forms, the scholarship of application focuses on utility to constituencies outside a discipline and, more important, to society in general. It is when the institutional reach extends to the lay public that researchers can expand their knowledge through practical application. This approach differs from the scholarship of discovery, where the research comes first and is followed by presentation and publication. In the scholarship of application, presentation is the focus, while the generation of new knowledge comes later in the process.

Thus, the objective of the scholarship of application is to serve the external environment of colleges and universities. Rice (1992) terms this form of scholarship the *scholarship of practice*. In 1996, Boyer termed it the *scholarship of engagement*. To avoid confusion, we label it the *scholarship of application*.

A handful of scholars advance perspectives on the meaning of such service to the external environment.

Service to the External Environment

Although scholars have focused extensively on Boyer's four domains of scholarship, the scholarship of application has received very little attention. The majority of writings deal with practical reasons why scholars need to focus on this area—for example, to avoid irrelevance (Boyer, 1990) or to counter the problems faced by the decline in public confidence of American universities (Boyer, 1996; Lynton, 1995). Johnston (1998) argues that all the domains of scholarship, including the scholarship of application, have been prioritized during different times based on the prevailing influences of the time, whether academic, sociological, economic, or political.

It is important to remember that although it is in the best interest of the professoriate and universities to foster relationships outside the university, it is just as important to retain autonomy. Boyer (1996) echoed this sentiment by stating that *town* is not *gown* and that the "university must vigorously protect its political and intellectual independence" (p. 15).

Throughout the history of higher education, universities have been called upon to solve urgent as well as less critical issues, and as problems were solved, public confidence in the American higher education system increased. It is not unrealistic to say that many in the professoriate agree it is time to give service higher priority in the profession once again. Knowledgeable faculty members, for example, can participate in policy analysis and program evaluation, curriculum revision, and the provision of more and better information for the public. Boyer believed that the most urgent issue during the time shortly before his death was the plight of children. He challenged academics not only to become actively engaged with school systems but also to take leading roles in the community surrounding the children.

Opportunities abound to help solve today's societal problems. Whether the scholarship of application will ever hold the same status as the scholarships of discovery or teaching remains a topic of much debate. Yet it is imperative that academics foster outside relationships not only to be of service but also to revise and enhance research, thereby increasing the public's confidence in higher education.

Shortly before his death, Boyer (1996) delivered a speech aimed at the scholarship of application or, as he called it at the time, the *scholarship of engagement*. Drawing on the history of higher education in general, he said, "The truth is that for more than 350 years, higher learning and the larger purposes of American society have been inextricably interlocked" (p. 11). Citing advances as diverse as the discovery of penicillin and the implementation of the Marshall Plan, which sent scholars overseas to promote economic and social progress, he discussed ways in which an institution's goals can be based on practical solutions to society's problems.

It is imperative that academics foster outside relationships not only to be of service but also to revise and enhance research, thereby increasing the public's confidence in higher education.

Although confidence in U.S. institutions of higher learning was strong during these times when academics were called upon to help solve problems small and large, Boyer believed that higher education's commitment to the scholarship of application had declined significantly. The tendency to promote work within a discipline and to condemn research that had become popularized or useful to nonacademics (Jacoby, 1987) had led to a disengagement of academic research from the lives of the public and to a decrease in the public's confidence in the higher education system as a whole. Boyer made the interesting point that while academics are disengaging themselves from the public view, those most in the public eye, such as politicians and reporters, often fail to call upon academics when discussing national issues or policies. Thus, although apathy for service may be an internal problem, an outcome is that external constituents no longer see a need to call on those most immersed in research for something as simple as gathering information.

Before the inception of the four domains of scholarship, Lynton (1983, 1995) wrote extensively about the scholarship of application or professional service, speaking about the institutional reach for external constituents. Like Boyer, he saw the scholarship of application as something faculty engage in when they go beyond their discipline and even the university to use their knowledge in some practical way to help others.

In 1994, Boyer noted that, more than ever before, "a commitment to service as well as teaching and research is needed" (1994a, p. A48). Because they have more intellectual talent than any other institution in our culture, colleges and universities must respond to society's challenges. Lynton went one step farther, saying that it is the increasing responsibility of the university to be instrumental in analyzing and applying new knowledge and in "making it rapidly useful to all sectors of society" (1983, p. 53; 1995, p. 1), taking the position that faculty members and universities should see that their knowledge, particularly original knowledge gained through research, is available and distributed to nonacademics so that it is immediately useful in solving society's problems. It goes beyond the town-gown relationship and is more than just working to improve the university's image in the town or city where it is located. When done for the benefit of others, the outcome can only be positive for the institution, the discipline, and the faculty member involved.

Another positive outcome is that through the scholarship of application, "knowledge is dynamic, constantly made fresh, and given new shape by its interaction with reality" (Lynton, 1995, p. 7). For this reason, the scholarship of application contributes substantially to the intellectual vitality of the university.

Service-Learning: A Special Case of the Scholarship of Application

A recent trend in colleges and universities has been to foster service among students to enhance their academic experiences. General student volunteer movements have been on campuses for generations but have never experienced true staying power until recently, with the inception of service-learning components in the curriculum. An outcome has been the increased visibility of faculty participation in these efforts that is vital to the staying power of an institution's commitment to public service (Levine, 1994; Zlotkowski, 1996). Although they are often not discussed in terms of Boyer's domains of scholarship, service-learning activities fall under the domain of the scholarship of application, as evidenced by Ramaley's plenary presentation (2000) at AAHE's 2000 Conference on Faculty Roles and Rewards. During her remarks, she discussed service-learning as a form of engaged learning that uses community issues for accomplishing educational goals.

A problem encountered by Zlotkowski (1996) in his analysis of service-learning and the academy is that although service-learning is gaining widespread popularity and although faculty members are incorporating it more often into their academic lives, the service movement has made "relatively little impact on the culture and consciousness of the academy in general, on the way in which its members define themselves and their work" (p. 23). He speculates about several reasons for this phenomenon, including a general gap in time between implementation and full acceptance. This outcome is congruent with the lag in full implementation of the scholarship of application among academics at various colleges and universities. Faculty members may be pursuing areas considered the scholarship of application, yet their efforts are often not given as much scholarly credit as the more traditional domains of discovery and teaching.

To counter the problem with acceptance of service-learning as academic, Zlotkowski (1996) calls for an increase in respect for service-learning as a "discipline-specific pedagogy" (p. 26). As such, an increase in the number of service presentations is necessary at national and regional conferences. Hand in hand with that increase is an increase in publications related to service-learning in academic journals. This focus toward more traditional scholarly activities is also one way to foster further acceptance of activities under the domain of the scholarship of application.

Documenting Professional Service

As a companion volume to *Making the Case for Professional Service,* Driscoll and Lynton (1999) published a guide to documenting professional service that looks at detailed examples of work documenting faculty professional service at various universities. They recommend that activities within the scholarship of application be documented as an ongoing process and that they be enhanced by collaborative reflection. If done consistently, the benefits of this type of reflection are far-reaching. One problem encountered by faculty engaged in this process is the tendency to think in traditional scholarly terms for outreach services, when the process is actually a new paradigm. This recommendation is a blending of the new with traditional components.

Service to the Institution

Boyer (1990, p. 22) also advances an internal focus for the scholarship of application. He points to the problematic status of service to the institution as a form of scholarship. He contends, however, that a clear differentiation must be made between activities of citizenship and of service. "To be considered scholarship, service activities must be tied directly to one's special field of knowledge and relate to, and flow directly out of, this professional activity" (Boyer, 1990, p. 22). Thus, service activities that use professional knowledge and skill in their performance fit the definition of scholarly activity (Braxton and Toombs, 1982; Pellino, Blackburn, and Boberg, 1984; Braxton and Bayer, 1986).

Various scholarly forms associated with the scholarship of application are exhibited in Appendix B. A crisper understanding of the scholarship of application results from a review of these scholarly forms.

The Function of the Scholarship of Application in the Scholarship Action System

Faculty engagement in the scholarship of application contributes to the maintenance and effectiveness of scholarship as a social action system. As discussed in the previous chapter, Paulsen and Feldman (1995) maintain that scholarship takes the form of a social action system. Four functional imperatives are necessary to sustain this system and make it effective, one of which is goal attainment. The functional imperative of goal attainment is enacted through the scholarship of application. An orientation toward the external environment characterizes goal attainment as a functional imperative (Parsons and Platt, 1973). Put differently, goal attainment entails the use of system resources to develop and achieve goals that relate to the external environment (Parsons and Platt, 1973). Because an objective of the scholarship of application is to solve problems of the external environment, Paulsen and Feldman regard the scholarship of application as performing the function of goal attainment for the scholarship action system. Because of the pragmatic values espoused by our society, engagement in the scholarship of application contributes to the well-being of scholarship as a system of social action (Paulsen and Feldman, 1995, p. 626). By applying disciplinary knowledge and skill to social and political problems, the scholarship of application contributes to the well-being of society (Paulsen and Feldman, 1995). Through such contributions, the scholarship of application acquires societal support for the scholarship social action system.

Moreover, Paulsen and Feldman assign the functional imperative of integration to the scholarship of academic citizenship. As a functional imperative, the subsystem of integration uses resources of a social action system to coordinate and control action both within this subsystem and with other subsystems. An internal focus on the social action system characterizes the functional imperative of integration. The scholarship of academic citizenship encompasses both institutional service activities and service activities performed for scholarly and professional associations. Accordingly, the scholarship of academic citizenship performs the function of integration. The internal focus of the scholarship of academic citizenship is directed toward service to the institution and to scholarly and professional associations.

Although not discussed by Paulsen and Feldman, scholarly activities reflective of the scholarship of application also play an integrative role in the scholarship action system. Such activities perform an integrative role if disciplinary knowledge and skill are applied in performing service to the college or university of academic appointment.

Faculty Engagement in the Scholarship of Application

This section pursues the set of questions advanced in the introduction to this volume pertaining to faculty engagement in the scholarship of application. As indicated in the introduction, we address these questions using our national study of faculty.

We use two scholarly forms to assess faculty engagement in the scholarship of application: unpublished scholarly outcomes, and publications. Unpublished scholarly outcomes serve as a proxy indicator of unpublished publicly observable scholarship (see "Contemporary Perspectives on Boyer" in the previous chapter). These two indices of scholarship engagement are measured as composites of the specific forms of scholarship displayed above. We show these forms in Appendix B.

General Levels of Engagement in the Scholarship of Application

Faculty levels of general career publication productivity are low (Finkelstein, 1984; Creswell, 1985; Fox, 1985). Boyer (1990) indicates that 41 percent of faculty have never published an article, monograph, or book during their careers. Finkelstein reports that 43 percent of faculty members have not published during the last two years (1984, p. 89, Table 5.1). Thus, two-year and career rates of publication performance show similar levels of publication activity.

In contrast to these general levels of publication activity, a higher proportion (57.1 percent) of faculty members report no publication activity for the scholarship of application during the previous three years (Appendix A, Table A.1). A strikingly higher level of engagement in the scholarship of application emerges, however, when unpublished scholarly outcomes associated with the scholarship of application are used as an indicator of performance: only one-fourth of faculty members report that they had not produced such scholarship during the previous three years (Table A.1).

> **A strikingly higher level of engagement in the scholarship of application emerges, however, when unpublished scholarly outcomes associated with the scholarship of application are used as an indicator of performance.**

Boyer's Prescriptions for Institutional Emphasis on the Scholarship of Application

Boyer (1990) holds that faculty members in doctoral-granting universities and comprehensive universities and colleges should engage themselves in the scholarship of application. Both publications and unpublished scholarly outcomes are used to assess the extent to which faculty members in these two types of institutions of higher education meet Boyer's expectations. We view Boyer's expectations for institutional domain emphasis as met if academics in doctoral-granting universities and comprehensive universities and colleges publish more scholarship focused on application or produce more unpublished scholarly outcomes oriented toward the scholarship of application than do academics in other types of colleges and universities (between institutional comparisons).

We also view Boyer's expectation met if faculty members in doctoral-granting universities and comprehensive universities and colleges publish more application-oriented scholarship or produce more unpublished scholarly outcomes focused on application than they do publications or unpublished scholarly outcomes focused on the scholarships of discovery, integration, or teaching (within institutional comparisons). Meeting either condition suffices.

The application of such criteria suggests that faculty members in doctoral-granting universities come close to meeting Boyer's expectations for their emphasis on engagement in the scholarship of application. That is, academics in doctoral-granting universities publish more scholarship focused on application than do their academic counterparts in teaching-oriented colleges and universities (Appendix A, Table A.2). They share similar levels of publication productivity associated with the scholarship of application with faculty members in research-oriented universities, however. Although faculty members in doctoral-granting universities publish more application-oriented scholarship than either scholarship reflective of integration or teaching, they nevertheless publish more discovery-based scholarship than they do scholarship directed toward application (Appendix A, Table A.3).

Like their colleagues in doctoral-granting universities, academics in comprehensive universities and colleges demonstrate progress toward meeting Boyer's expectations for their engagement in the scholarship of application. Specifically, they publish more within the scholarship of application than within the scholarship of teaching but exhibit similar levels of publication productivity for application-focused and integration-oriented scholarship (Table A.3). Like their counterparts in doctoral-granting universities, academics in comprehensive universities and colleges also publish more discovery-oriented scholarship than they do within the other three domains (Table A.3).

Mirroring Institutional Differences in General Publication Productivity

The introduction to this volume raises a general question: Does faculty publication productivity within each of Boyer's four domains of scholarship across different types of colleges and universities mirror the general level of publication productivity exhibited across different types of colleges and universities? For publications associated with the scholarship of application, our findings indicate that the differences in faculty publication productivity within the domain of the scholarship of application parallel the structure of institutional differences found by scholars using general indices of publication productivity (Fulton and Trow, 1974; Finkelstein, 1984; Creswell, 1985; Blackburn and Lawrence, 1995). Such a structure of institutional differences takes the form of faculty publication productivity being the greatest in research and doctoral-granting universities.

Academic Disciplines and Engagement in the Scholarship of Application

The formulations focusing on differences among academic disciplines found in the introduction to this volume suggest that faculty performance levels within the domain of the scholarship of application may vary across different academic disciplines. Such differences may occur between high and low paradigmatic academic fields.

Scholarship focusing on application demonstrates disciplinary differences (Appendix A, Table A.4). Academic sociologists (low paradigmatic) accomplish more unpublished scholarly outcomes in the form of application than do academic chemists (high paradigmatic) and historians (low paradigmatic). In contrast, academic chemists generate more publications reflective of the scholarship of application than the other three academic disciplines.

Unlike the research findings reviewed by Braxton and Hargens (1996) that suggest distinctions between high and low paradigmatic disciplines across a range of phenomena, disciplinary paradigmatic development appears not to account for the disciplinary differences we observed for publications and unpublished scholarly outcomes toward application. The basic tasks and ideology of a discipline may account for these differences in performance. For example, Becher (1989) points out that some specialties in chemistry focus on the commercial applications of their research.

Faculty Characteristics and Engagement in the Scholarship of Application

Research indicates that various faculty characteristics influence their research role performance (Creswell, 1985; Fox, 1985; Blackburn and Lawrence, 1995;

Creamer, 1998). These characteristics include gender, race/ethnicity, prestige of the doctoral program, tenure, and age. Do such characteristics affect faculty engagement in the scholarship of application? Do such individual characteristics influence faculty engagement in the scholarship of application in the same way that they influence general publication productivity?

Gender. Gender affects faculty publication performance in the scholarship of application domain but not in the production of unpublished scholarly outcomes of this domain (Appendix A, Table A.5). More specifically, male academics tend to produce slightly more publications associated with the scholarship of application than do female academics. This finding resonates with the conclusions of scholars who have reviewed research on factors that influence general publication productivity (Creswell, 1985; Fox, 1985; Creamer, 1998) but conflicts with the findings of Blackburn and Lawrence (1995). The failure of gender to wield an influence on the production of unpublished scholarly outcomes is, however, consistent with Blackburn and Lawrence's findings (1995).

Race/Ethnicity. A faculty member's race or ethnicity exerts little or no influence on publication productivity and the production of unpublished scholarly outcomes within the domain of the scholarship of application (Table A.5). Based on the findings of Blackburn and Lawrence (1995) and Creamer's conclusion (1998) from her review of research that race is not a reliable predictor of publication productivity, our findings are not surprising. These findings are nonetheless consistent with such previous research.

Prestige of the Doctoral Program. From Fox's review (1985) of literature on the influence of quality/prestige of the doctoral program on publication productivity, we might anticipate a positive relationship between prestige of the doctoral program and faculty engagement in the three forms reflective of the scholarship of application. Prestige of a faculty member's doctoral program, however, negatively affects faculty accomplishment of unpublished scholarly outcomes (Table A.5). Publication productivity, however, is not affected by the prestige of a faculty member's doctoral program (Table A.5).

Tenure. Creswell (1985) concludes from his review of research on faculty publication productivity that tenure exerts little or no influence on general publication performance. Likewise, holding tenure wields little or no influence on the production of unpublished scholarly outcomes and publications that hold an orientation toward application (Table A.5).

Professional Age. As faculty professional age increases, their level of publication performance within the domain of the scholarship of application decreases (Table A.5). This finding supports Finkelstein's conclusion (1984) that publication productivity decreases with age. Professional age wields little or no influence on faculty production of application-oriented unpublished scholarly outcomes, however (Table A.5). Such a finding bolsters Fox's conclusion (1985) and Creswell's conclusion (1985) that age and research performance are so weakly related that policy should not be predicated on this relationship.

The Scholarship of Discovery

THE STANDARD FORM OF SCHOLARSHIP is discovery (Boyer, 1990), whose aim is to acquire knowledge for its own sake. The testing and generation of theory is also an essential facet of the scholarship of discovery.

According to Johnston (1998), "Boyer insisted in the scholarship of discovery, or research, as a pervasive process of intellectual excitement rather than just a concern with outcomes in the form of new knowledge" (p. 253). This statement follows Boyer's resolve that discovery is a way to avoid stagnation. Rather than research as something rote and mundane, the scholarship of discovery challenges scholars to maintain an enthusiasm about their work and the contribution it will make to the profession. Because the nature of research requires researchers to be fully informed of developments in their field, discovery keeps the individual informed of new knowledge. It also results, however, in an addition to that body of knowledge, generally through presentation and publication.

The academic profession ascribes high value to originality in scholarship (Hagstrom, 1965; Gaston, 1971; Merton, 1957). High value accrues to an original discovery, because an important aspect of the world is identified and demonstrated for the first time (Hagstrom, 1965). As such, originality in discovery results in recognition by colleagues for making such a contribution to knowledge. Such recognition results in high standing in an academic discipline for the individual academic (Braxton, 1993). More specifically, recognition by colleagues takes such forms as election to office in scholarly and professional associations, appointment to governmental advisory boards, and appointment to journal editorial boards (Braxton, 1986). Reference and citations to published work are additional forms of recognition by colleagues (Braxton and Bayer, 1986). For these reasons, the scholarship of discovery stands as the preeminent domain of scholarship. Thus, the traditional scholarship assessment template (refereed journal articles, scholarly books, book chapters, and number of citations) provides the appropriate basis for the appraisal of faculty performance in this domain of scholarship (Braxton and Del Favero, forthcoming).

A provocative aspect of the scholarship of discovery is the lack of attention in the literature to this domain of scholarship. Unlike the scholarship of teaching, which has generated much scholarly attention to clarifying its objectives, attention given to discovery is distinctly lacking.

Appendix B displays scholarly forms associated with the scholarship of discovery. These forms bring further clarity to the objectives of the scholarship of discovery.

The Function of the Scholarship of Discovery in the Scholarship Action System

As previously indicated, faculty scholarship constitutes a social action system (Paulsen and Feldman, 1995). The continuation and effectiveness of this system depends on adequate performance of four functions. Pattern maintenance stands as one of the four functional imperatives necessary for the survival and effectiveness of a social action system (Parsons and Platt, 1973). Pattern maintenance develops and sustains patterns of ideas, values, and beliefs that form the basic frame of reference for all action in a given social system (Paulsen and Feldman, 1995).

Paulsen and Feldman designate the scholarship of discovery as performing the function of pattern maintenance for the scholarship action system. They do so because the creation and advancement of knowledge serve to develop and maintain the symbolic values, ideas, and beliefs that are fundamental to scholarship and the scholarship action system.

Faculty Engagement in the Scholarship of Discovery

This section appraises faculty engagement in the scholarship of discovery, using publications associated with this domain as an indicator of engagement. The various forms of publications we use are presented in Appendix B. Publications as an index of engagement in the scholarship of discovery are measured as a composite.

General Levels of Engagement in the Scholarship of Discovery

Faculty publication productivity within the scholarship of discovery sharply contrasts with the picture of career and two-year general publication productivity portrayed by Finkelstein (1984), Creswell (1985), Fox (1985), and Boyer (1990). Specifically, the vast majority of faculty members (72.4 percent) report one or more publications associated with the scholarship of discovery during the previous three years (Appendix A, Table A.1). This proportion stands in notable contrast to the 43 percent of faculty who published nothing during the previous two years (Finkelstein, 1984) and the 41 percent of faculty who published nothing during their academic careers (Boyer, 1990).

Boyer's Prescriptions for Institutional Emphasis on the Scholarship of Discovery

Boyer (1990) held that some faculty in all types of colleges and universities might pursue the scholarship of discovery. He asserted, however, that faculty members in research and doctoral-granting universities should engage in the scholarship of discovery. We assess Boyer's expectations for institutional domain emphasis achieved if faculty members in research-oriented and doctoral-granting universities publish more scholarship focused on discovery than do academics in other types of colleges and universities. We also view Boyer's expectations as attained if faculty members in research-oriented and doctoral-granting universities publish more discovery-oriented scholarship than publications focused on the scholarships of application, integration, or teaching (within institutional comparisons). Meeting either criterion suffices.

Academics in research-oriented universities match Boyer's expectations by both of the above criteria. That is, faculty members in research universities tend to publish more discovery-oriented scholarship than do their faculty counterparts in doctoral-granting universities and in more teaching-oriented colleges and universities, such as comprehensive universities and colleges–I and liberal arts colleges–I and –II (Table A.2). Moreover, academics in research universities publish more within the discovery domain of scholarship than they publish within the scholarly domains of application, integration, and teaching (Table A.3).

Doctoral-granting university faculty members also meet Boyer's expectations for an emphasis on the scholarship of discovery, given that they publish more discovery-oriented scholarship than they publish scholarship focused on application, integration, or teaching (Table A.3).

Mirroring Institutional Differences in General Publication Productivity

Does faculty publication productivity in each of Boyer's four domains of scholarship across different types of colleges and universities mirror the general level of publication productivity across different types of colleges and universities? This section concentrates specifically on this question for the scholarship of discovery.

Research reporting variation in faculty general publication productivity across different types of colleges and universities (Fulton and Trow, 1974; Finkelstein, 1984; Boyer, 1990; Blackburn and Lawrence, 1995) suggests that faculty in research-oriented universities exhibit greater levels of general publication productivity than their academic colleagues in other types of colleges and universities. Faculty publication productivity associated with the scholarship of discovery parallels the pattern of institutional differences in general publication productivity found in the research literature (Table A.2).

Academic Disciplines and Engagement in the Scholarship of Discovery

As discussed in the introduction to this volume, the differences between disciplines of high and low paradigmatic development are "profound and extensive" (Braxton and Hargens, 1996). Thus, faculty engagement in the scholarship of discovery may also vary across different academic disciplines. Such differences may occur between disciplines classified according to Biglan (1973) as pure-hard paradigmatic and pure-soft paradigmatic.

Faculty members in pure-hard (biology and chemistry) paradigmatic disciplines, however, differ little from their academic counterparts in pure-soft paradigmatic academic fields (history and sociology) in their publication of discovery-oriented scholarship (Table A.4). Such a finding conflicts with the body of literature reviewed by Braxton and Hargens (1996) regarding the role of disciplinary paradigmatic development in differentiating the behavior of college and university faculty members.

Faculty Characteristics and Engagement in the Scholarship of Discovery

Such faculty characteristics as gender, race/ethnicity, prestige of the doctoral-granting department, tenure, and professional age exert an influence on general publication productivity research role performance (Creswell, 1985; Fox, 1985; Creamer, 1998; Blackburn and Lawrence, 1995). Do such characteristics influence publication productivity of the scholarship of discovery? Do such faculty characteristics influence faculty publication productivity associated with the scholarship of discovery in ways that resemble their influence on general publication productivity?

Gender. Gender wields a small influence on publication productivity associated with the scholarship of discovery. Specifically, male academics tend to publish more discovery-based scholarship than do female academics (Table A.5). The small influence of gender on publication within the scholarship of discovery domain resonates with the conclusions of scholars who have reviewed studies reporting the effects of gender on publication productivity (Creswell, 1985; Fox, 1985; Creamer, 1998).

Race/Ethnicity. A faculty member's race or ethnic group fails to influence publication productivity associated with the scholarship of discovery (Table A.5). This pattern of findings is consistent with the findings of

Blackburn and Lawrence (1995) and with Creamer's conclusion (1998) that race does not predict publication productivity (p. 19).

A faculty member's race or ethnic group fails to influence publication productivity associated with the scholarship of discovery.

Prestige of Doctoral Program. Fox (1985) notes from her extensive review of research that publication productivity is directly or indirectly influenced by the quality/prestige of a faculty member's doctoral program. Such an influence may wane over the course of an academic career (Creswell, 1985). The prestige of a faculty member's doctoral program exerts a small positive effect on publication productivity within the domain of the scholarship of discovery (Table A.5), thus echoing Fox's observation (1985).

Tenure. Holding academic tenure slightly affects scholarship of discovery publication productivity of faculty members. Put differently, tenured faculty tend to publish a bit more in the scholarship of discovery domain than do their untenured faculty colleagues (Table A.5). This finding contradicts Creswell's conclusion (1985) from his review of research on the correlates of publication productivity that tenure wields little or no influence on publication performance.

Professional Age. Finkelstein (1984) concludes from the studies he reviewed that publication productivity decreases with age, whereas Fox (1985) notes from her review that age and productivity are weakly related at best. She cautions "against any educational policy on the basis of age and productivity relationship per se" (p. 262). Creswell (1985) concurs with Fox's assessment (1985) of the influence of age on publication productivity.

Professional age exerts a modest, negative effect on the publication of discovery-oriented scholarship, however (Table A.5). Put differently, as faculty professional age increases, publication of discovery-focused scholarship decreases. It should be noted that we did not use chronological age as did Finkelstein (1984), Creswell (1985), and Fox (1985). We define professional age as the number of years elapsed since the receipt of the doctoral degree.

The Scholarship of Integration

THE SCHOLARSHIP OF INTEGRATION has received the least amount of scholarly attention of Boyer's four domains. An ERIC search of the scholarship of integration resulted in only eight references, while the scholarship of teaching generated 179 mentions. In fact, Rice (1998) holds that the scholarship of integration is the most poorly developed of the four domains and has made the least progress.

Clearly, the scholarship of discovery is the best regarded and rewarded of the four domains. The scholarship of teaching has been highly provocative and the featured attraction of numerous national conferences on teaching and learning. The American Association for Higher Education recently held a national conference focusing on the scholarship of application/engagement. Why is the scholarship of integration so poorly developed relative to the other three scholarly domains?

One possible argument for the diminished status of the scholarship of integration is the dominant role that each of the other three domains has played at various times in the evolution of the American system of higher education. For instance, the earliest American universities followed the "colonial college" model and highly valued the teaching professor (Bell and Gordon, 1999). Upon assuming the presidency of Harvard College in 1869, Charles W. Eliot proclaimed "the prime business of American professors must be regular and assiduous class teaching" (Boyer, 1990, p. 4). Clearly, the scholarship of teaching was at one time the dominant domain.

Later, with passage of the Morrill Act in 1862, many comprehensive land-grant institutions began to emerge. These institutions were established to improve the quality of life for people across the country by applying knowledge and research to solving everyday problems and concerns (Lidstone, Hacker, and Oien, 1996). With the emergence of land-grant institutions, the scholarship of application took on more importance, as these universities were created to improve agricultural practices and to share this information with farmers across the country.

Eventually, the Germanic model of scholarship began to emerge. By 1895, William Rainey Harper, the president of the newly formed University of Chicago, required "each appointee to sign an agreement that his promotion in rank and salary would depend chiefly upon his research productivity" (Boyer, 1990, p. 9). By the end of World War II, university faculty began to be hired as teachers but were clearly being evaluated as researchers (Bell and Gordon, 1999). The research universities and their faculty became the yardstick by which all institutions would be measured (Boyer, 1990). For most of the twentieth century, scholarship essentially was narrowly defined as the scholarship of discovery. It has been and largely remains the dominant domain. The extension of the frontiers of knowledge through the scholarship of discovery is not enough to fully capture the mosaic of faculty talents, however (Rice, 1991).

What Is the Scholarship of Integration?

The scholarship of integration is serious disciplined work that gives new meaning and perspective to isolated facts, often overcoming the fragmentation of the disciplines to instead see the connectedness of things (Boyer, 1990). This connectedness "is what the educator contemplates to the limit of his capacity. No human capacity is great enough to permit a vision of the world as simple, but if the educator does not aim at the vision no one else will, and the consequences are dire when no one else does" (Van Doren, 1959, p. 115).

Boyer suggests that it is the responsibility of the university to "help students better understand the interdependent nature of our world" (1990, p. 77). Scholars need not only to generate new knowledge but also to integrate ideas connecting thought to action. It is higher education's quest "to build bridges across the disciplines, and connect the campus to the larger world" (Boyer, 1990, p. 77).

The scholarship of integration often involves doing research at the boundaries where fields converge. It thus emphasizes the importance of interdisciplinary research, which often involves research in areas that have been marginalized in academia, such as women's studies or other integrative studies (Park, 1996). The scholarship of integration seeks to interpret, draw together, and bring new insight to original research. "Scholars are needed with a capacity to synthesize, to look for new relationships between the parts and the whole, to relate the past and future to the present, and to ferret out patterns of meaning that cannot be seen through traditional disciplinary lenses" (Rice, 1991, p. 13).

The scholarship of integration also means interpretation, "fitting one's own research or the research of others into larger intellectual patterns" (Boyer, 1990, p. 19). New knowledge from original research is less useful if it is not integrated into a larger body of concepts and facts (Halpern and others, 1998). Book reviews, meta-analyses, textbooks, and a book in the popular press addressing a disciplinary/interdisciplinary topic are all examples of scholarship involving the integration of knowledge. For instance, *John Adams* by David McCullough has been on *The New York Times* best-seller list for months and yet would not be considered scholarship if only the narrowly defined scholarship of discovery were considered. This work is clearly scholarly, however, and falls under the umbrella of the scholarship of integration.

The scholarship of integration requires scholars who give meaning to isolated facts, illuminate data in a revealing way, make connections across the discipline, and synthesize the knowledge of the discipline. It is closely related to the scholarship of discovery but instead involves research in "overlapping academic neighborhoods" (Polanyi, 1967, p. 72). The key question for this domain is what the findings mean (Huber, 1998).

Ruscio (1987) has found the scholarship of integration to be particularly alive in the selective liberal arts colleges, largely, he believes, because of the horizontal orientation of these colleges that encourages academics from various disciplines to interact. He found the selective liberal arts colleges to be far less bureaucratic than the vertically organized universities. Presumably, a department of seventy-two sociologists at a larger university would likely not have relationships with faculty members from other disciplines as strong as those at a small liberal arts college with only two academics in the department.

Although the scholarship of integration has never been the dominant operating domain in the system of higher education, a number of pedagogical revolutions are occurring that may boost the status of the scholarship of integration. First, collaboration is a growing phenomenon in higher education that dovetails well with the scholarship of integration (Baldwin and Austin, 1995). Faculty members working collaboratively often can produce more creative work than they could working alone. Boyer suggests that faculty "feel the need to move beyond traditional disciplinary boundaries, communicate with colleagues in other fields, and discover patterns that connect" (1990, p. 20).

The second piece to the pedagogical revolution is the expansion of technology throughout the academy. Through the Internet, fax machines, telephones, and e-mail, new professional relationships can be forged and graduate school ties maintained. In addition, discussion groups among scholars can be created to eliminate the isolation and specialization that scholars once felt (Dunn and Zaremba, 1997). These technological advances have assisted in breaking the barriers to isolation and have opened the doors to more integrative scholarship.

In fact, Boyer, just one year before his death, mentioned that the scholarship of integration was the one domain most relevant to our future (Johnston, 1998). "I am convinced that in the twenty-first century, at the very time that we talk about specialization, we will begin to see patterns of great convergence. I think the challenge of the next century is not only the discovery of knowledge, but fitting those discoveries into a larger pattern and perspective" (Boyer, 1994b, p. 118). That same year, Boyer wrote about the emergence of a different kind of educational institution, one he called the *New American College* (Zlotkowski, 1997). "This New American College would organize cross-disciplinary institutes around pressing social issues. The New American College, as a connected institution, would be committed to improving, in a very intentional way, the human condition" (Boyer, 1994a, p. A48). Although the remaining three domains of scholarship have had their day, the future may well belong to the scholarship of integration.

We present scholarly forms reflective of the scholarship of integration in Appendix B. The objectives of the scholarship of integration domain become clearer with a review of these forms of scholarship.

The Function of the Scholarship of Integration in the Scholarship Action System

Scholarship takes the form of a social action system that requires adequate performance of four functions: adaptation, goal attainment, pattern maintenance, and integration. Unlike for the scholarships of discovery, application, and teaching, Paulsen and Feldman (1995) do not assign a singular functional role in the scholarship action system to the scholarship of integration. Rather, they contend that the role played by the scholarship of integration serves the functional imperatives of adaptation, pattern maintenance, and goal attainment. Because of its scholarly objectives, Paulsen and Feldman carefully point out that Boyer's scholarship of integration does not perform the functional role of integration in the scholarship action system. Instead, they assign the functional role of integration to academic citizenship or the internal service orientation of Boyer's scholarship of application.

> **Scholarship takes the form of a social action system that requires adequate performance of four functions: adaptation, goal attainment, pattern maintenance, and integration.**

Faculty Engagement in the Scholarship of Integration

This section discusses the questions advanced in the introduction to this volume. This set of questions focuses on the level of faculty engagement in the scholarship of integration. As for previous domains of scholarship, we present findings from our study that address these questions. We use two indices of faculty scholarship engagement: unpublished scholarly outcomes and publications. We use unpublished scholarly outcomes as a proxy for unpublished publicly observable scholarship. These scholarly forms are discussed in more detail in the previous chapter. Appendix B displays the specific types of publications and unpublished scholarly outcomes we used in our measurement of faculty performance in this domain.

General Levels of Engagement in the Scholarship of Integration

Like for publication productivity associated with the scholarship of discovery described earlier, a clear contrast with career and two-year rates of general publication inactivity identified by Finkelstein (1984), Creswell (1985), and Fox (1985) exists for faculty engagement in the scholarship of integration. Specifically, a higher level of publication activity within the scholarship of integration exists, as fewer than 30 percent of faculty members report no publications reflective of the scholarship of integration during the previous three years (Appendix A, Table A.1). A similar level of activity in the production of integration-oriented scholarship that appears as an unpublished scholarly outcome also is apparent, as slightly more than one-third (34.7 percent) of faculty report no such scholarship (Table A.1). These proportions stand in contrast with 43 percent of faculty during the previous two years (Finkelstein, 1984) and 41 percent of faculty during their careers who register no publications (Boyer, 1990).

Boyer's Prescriptions for Institutional Emphasis on the Scholarship of Integration

Boyer (1990) asserts that academics in liberal arts colleges and in comprehensive universities and colleges should engage in the scholarship of integration. This assertion echoes Ruscio's view (1987) that the scholarship of integration characterizes the scholarship of liberal arts colleges, especially highly selective liberal arts colleges. We view Boyer's expectations for institutional emphasis on the scholarship of integration as fulfilled if academics in comprehensive universities and colleges and liberal arts colleges publish more scholarship focused on integration or produce more unpublished scholarly outcomes reflective of the scholarship of integration than do academics in other types of colleges and universities (between institutional comparisons). We also view Boyer's expectations as satisfied if faculty members in liberal arts colleges and comprehensive universities and colleges publish more integration-oriented scholarship or produce more unpublished scholarly outcomes focused on integration than publications or unpublished scholarly outcomes focused on the scholarships of application, discovery, or teaching (within institutional comparisons). Meeting either condition suffices.

Faculty members in more selective liberal arts colleges and in comprehensive universities and colleges approximate Boyer's prescriptions for institutional emphasis on the scholarship of integration. More specifically, faculty members in both comprehensive universities and colleges and more selective liberal arts colleges publish more scholarship of integration than they publish scholarship of teaching (Table A.3). Academics in less selective liberal arts colleges, however, do not match Boyer's expectations for engagement in the scholarship of integration by either criterion (Tables A.2 and A.3). Nonetheless, academics in more and less selective liberal arts colleges and comprehensive universities and colleges publish more scholarship of discovery than scholarship of integration (Table A.3).

Mirroring Institutional Differences in General Publication Productivity

Does faculty publication productivity within each of Boyer's four domains of scholarship found across different types of colleges and universities mirror the level of general publication productivity found across different types of colleges and universities? Given that faculty in research and doctoral-granting universities publish more integration-oriented scholarship than do their counterparts in teaching-oriented colleges and universities, faculty publication productivity in the scholarship of integration mirrors the structure of general faculty publication productivity across institutional type: academics in research and doctoral-granting universities publish more than do their faculty colleagues in other types of collegiate institutions (Table A.2).

Academic Disciplines and Engagement in the Scholarship of Integration

The research reviewed in the introduction to this volume indicates that faculty members in high paradigmatic disciplines differ from academics in low paradigmatic disciplines on a wide range of phenomena (Braxton and Hargens, 1996). Accordingly, we might expect the level of engagement in the scholarship of integration to vary between faculty members in disciplines of high and low paradigmatic development.

Such differences between high and low paradigmatic disciplines occur for both publication productivity and the production of unpublished scholarly outcomes reflective of the scholarship of integration. To elaborate, academics in the discipline of history register higher levels of achievement of unpublished scholarly outcomes than do their counterparts in the disciplines of biology and chemistry (Table A.4). Moreover, academic sociologists achieve a higher level of unpublished scholarly outcomes focused on integration than do their faculty colleagues in chemistry.

Academic historians also publish more of such scholarship than do their faculty colleagues in the disciplines of biology, chemistry, and sociology (Table A.4). Furthermore, sociology faculty members publish more of such scholarship than do academics in the disciplines of biology and chemistry. Chemistry and biology are high paradigmatic disciplines, whereas history and sociology are low paradigmatic disciplines.

Faculty Characteristics and Engagement in the Scholarship of Integration

The introduction to this volume raises two questions: Do such characteristics also influence the performance of the scholarship of integration? Do such characteristics influence faculty engagement in the scholarship of integration in the same way that they influence general publication productivity?

Gender. Gender has a small effect on faculty production of publications oriented toward integration. Specifically, male academics publish slightly more than do women academics (Table A.5). This finding is consistent with the conclusions of scholars who have reviewed research on the influence of gender on general publication productivity (Creswell, 1985; Fox, 1985; Creamer, 1998), and it is consistent with institutional type, academic discipline, and the other faculty characteristics held constant.

The production of unpublished scholarly outcomes, however, is unaffected by gender (Table A.5). This finding is consistent with research by Blackburn and Lawrence (1995), who found that general publication productivity is unaffected by gender.

Race/Ethnicity. From her review of research, Creamer (1998) found that race does not predict general publication productivity (p. 19). Our findings support Creamer's conclusion when publications are used as an index of engagement in the scholarship of integration. Specifically, being Caucasian, African American, or Asian fails to influence such publication productivity when institutional type, academic discipline, and other faculty characteristics are controlled (Table A.5). African-American academics tend, however, to produce slightly more scholarship in the form of unpublished scholarly outcomes than do faculty members of other racial/ethnic groups (Table A.5).

Prestige of Doctoral Program. The prestige of a faculty member's doctoral program exerts little or no effect on the number of publications and the accomplishment of unpublished scholarly outcomes oriented toward integration (Table A.5). Fox's conclusion (1985) that general publication productivity is directly or indirectly influenced by the prestige of a faculty member's doctoral program receives some support from this finding.

Tenure. Creswell (1985) concluded from his review of research that tenure exerts little or no influence on general publication productivity. Our research supports Creswell's conclusion, as the holding of tenure affects neither the production of unpublished scholarly outcomes nor publications associated with the scholarship of integration (Table A.5).

Professional Age. Professional age exerts little or no influence on the generation of unpublished scholarly outcomes or publication productivity within the scholarship of integration (Table A.5). Fox's view (1985) that no educational policy should be predicated on the relationship between general faculty publication productivity and age finds backing in this pattern of findings.

The Scholarship of Teaching

NONE OF BOYER'S FOUR DOMAINS of scholarship have received as much attention and as little consensus as the scholarship of teaching. In fact, an ERIC search for the scholarship of teaching produced 179 references, compared with only 29 mentions for the other three domains combined.

Why has so much been written about the scholarship of teaching and so little about the scholarships of application, integration, and discovery? One possible explanation is that the other three domains simply are not as provocative as the scholarship of teaching. Scholars generally agree about what Boyer meant by the scholarship of application, the scholarship of discovery, and the scholarship of integration. But the scholarship of teaching has been strongly contested, with various scholars refusing to bend toward consensus.

> **None of Boyer's four domains of scholarship have received as much attention and as little consensus as the scholarship of teaching.**

Any discussion of the scholarship of teaching should begin with Ernest Boyer and his *Scholarship Reconsidered* (1990). Boyer's first statement in his seminal work regarding the scholarship of teaching is that "the work of the professor becomes consequential only as it is understood by others" (p. 23). Was Boyer referring to the professor's work being understood by the students in the classroom, or was Boyer suggesting that it is only consequential when the professor's work in the classroom is understood by other academics through published manuscripts or other methods of peer review? The answer to this question is essentially the crux of the debate among scholars studying the scholarship of teaching.

Boyer suggested that as a scholarly enterprise, teaching involves three elements. It begins with what the teacher knows. Professors must be well informed, intellectually alive, widely read, and steeped in the knowledge of their disciplines. This first step requires enormous work and serious study and is foundational to scholarly teaching. Second, as a scholarly enterprise, teaching must be a dynamic endeavor where the professor must build bridges between the understanding that the professor possesses and students' learning. In this situation, pedagogical procedures must be carefully considered, continuously examined, and directly related to the subject being taught. Finally, faculty must also continue to be learners. Teaching means transforming knowledge and extending it as well. It is not enough to simply transmit knowledge (Boyer, 1990).

Boyer went on to define scholarship as the process through which knowledge is acquired, noting that knowledge can be acquired through research (discovery), synthesis (integration), practice (application), and teaching. But for teaching to be considered on a par with research, it must be vigorously assessed from at least three sources of assessment: self-assessment, peer assessment, and student assessment.

In self-assessment, the professor must figure out what works and what does not work in the classroom. In addition, the professor must identify barriers to overcome and initiate steps to improve the process. In fact, Boyer thought it was appropriate to have faculty prepare a written statement regarding class goals, procedures, and course outlines and provide copies of examinations and other evaluation processes.

The second source of assessment is peer assessment. Boyer strongly believed in the importance of a serious, systematic approach to the evaluation of teaching by one's colleagues. He believed that teaching was too important to be a private act and that faculty should work together to establish criteria for assessing good teaching. Through this process, classrooms would be opened up and faculty colleagues would be encouraged to move freely in and out of classrooms. He even suggested the possibility of *teaching circles,* in which a small group of interested faculty could participate in ongoing conversations to discuss pedagogical procedures that they found to be effective.

The final source of assessment Boyer mentions is student assessment. Boyer believed that this process should include former as well as current students. For this process to work, students would need to be well prepared to perform this important evaluation, and the procedures would need to be carefully designed.

These notions capture Boyer's formulations regarding the scholarship of teaching when *Scholarship Reconsidered* was published in 1990. He lived only five years after its publication, and most of the evolution of the scholarship of teaching has occurred since his death.

Perspectives on the Scholarship of Teaching

In *The New American Scholar,* Rice (1991) argues that the scholarship of teaching was difficult to discuss because an appropriate language did not exist for articulating this concept. Scholarship and teaching had always been thought of as antithetical. These two activities were interlocked in a zero-sum game where they always competed for an academic's time and attention. Rice, on the other hand, wanted to change this perception, arguing that "quality teaching requires substantive scholarship that builds on, but is distinct from, original research" (1991, p. 14).

Rice believes the scholarship of teaching has an integrity of its own but is deeply embedded in the scholarship of discovery, the scholarship of application, and the scholarship of integration. According to Rice, the scholarship of teaching has three distinct elements: synoptic capacity, pedagogical content knowledge, and what we know about learning. Rice describes synoptic capacity as "the ability to draw the strands of a field together in a way that provides both coherence and meaning, to place what is known in context and open the way for connection to be made between the knower and the known" (Rice, 1991, p. 15). In short, synoptic capacity involves using academic content knowledge to draw together various areas of an academic discipline and placing those concepts in the larger context of that discipline (Ronkowski, 1993).

Rice's second element of the scholarship of teaching is pedagogical content knowledge—a concept that has received considerable attention in the literature (Paulsen, 2001; Centra, 2001; Ronkowski, 1993; Rice, 1991; Shulman, 1987). Essentially, pedagogical content knowledge is the capacity to figure out how to help students learn through a special expertise in using simulations, metaphors, and examples. Rice describes it as "the capacity to represent a subject in ways that transcend the split between intellectual substance and teaching process" (1991, p. 15).

Rice's final element of the scholarship of teaching is what he refers to as "what we know about learning." It involves scholarly inquiry into how students make meaning out of what the teacher says and does. Ronkowski (1993) refers to it as being able to recognize the diversity of student learning characteristics. It is the ability to understand general learning principles and to possess knowledge about various stages of student cognition. In fact, Ronkowski draws a sharp distinction between the scholarly professionals who make careful use of principles and theoretical frameworks in conducting their classes and the do-it-yourselfers who fly by the seat of their pants (Ronkowski, 1993).

Rice concludes by reminding us that all faculty should remain students throughout their careers. They should remain scholars in the broadest sense, "deepening their preferred approaches to knowing but constantly pressing, and being pressed by, peers to enlarge their scholarly capacities and encompass other—often contrary—ways of knowing" (1991, p. 16).

The Teaching Portfolio

In a monograph titled *The Teaching Portfolio: Capturing the Scholarship in Teaching,* Edgerton, Hutchings, and Quinlan (1991) note that the scholarship of teaching is difficult to grasp but that it does have many of the same characteristics as other more traditional scholarly activities. For instance, "teaching relies on a base of expertise, a 'scholarly knowing' that needs to and can be identified, made public and evaluated" (p. 1). They believe that faculty are responsible for monitoring their own scholarship of teaching and that the teaching portfolio is the most effective tool for uncovering this scholarship. Seldin (1991) sees the teaching portfolio "as a factual description of a professor's major strengths and teaching achievements" and thinks the portfolio should be carried around to showcase special faculty talents in much the same way an architect, artist, designer, or photographer might display his or her best work (p. 3). The important point to remember is that Edgerton, Hutchings, and Quinlan expect individual faculty members to police their own scholarship of teaching. Although the portfolio could be made public for evaluation, Edgerton, Hutchings, and Quinlan still think of the scholarship of teaching as a private act.

Diamond (1993) takes a broader approach to the word *scholarship,* suggesting that any faculty work would be recognized as scholarship in most disciplines if it meets six criteria: requires a high level of discipline-related expertise, breaks new ground or is innovative, can be replicated or elaborated, can be documented, can be peer received, and has an impact on those directly affected by the work. Diamond does not suggest that this faculty work has to be peer reviewed or documented to be considered scholarship. Simply the possibility of replicating, documenting, or having the scholarly activity peer reviewed is sufficient to warrant the word *scholarship.*

Post-Boyer Perspectives

Everything presented in this review thus far occurred before Boyer's death. The scholarship of teaching as it was understood in 1995 was within the grasp of many academics. But that notion quickly began to change.

Classroom Research
Cross (1998) believes that the scholarship of teaching is implemented through classroom research but not through classroom assessment. Although the two have often been thought of as interchangeable, classroom assessment addresses the "what" of student learning, classroom research the "how" and "why." Why did students respond as they did? How can the material be presented more effectively? Classroom research attempts to answer these questions by turning classrooms into laboratories.

Cross (1998) believes that to maximize student learning, teachers have to know more about how students learn and students must participate in knowing more about the process. She notes that teachers are far too busy to read refereed journal articles about someone else's classroom experience that may or may not be applicable to the students in their own classrooms. With classroom research, academics deal with a relevant classroom, relevant students, a relevant discipline, and relevant concerns. Academics do not need a sample size of several hundred to ensure statistical significance. In fact, Cross believes that an interview with a single student or a small focus group may be much more valuable and enlightening.

Classroom research may or may not be published. Its primary requirement is that it benefit teachers and students. Classroom researchers are interested in studying variables that can be altered, such as teaching techniques or study strategies, as they learn about learning. Although classroom research may not be published, it nevertheless should be credible and worthy of colleagues' attention. "Teachers employ the scholarship of discovery when they use classroom research to inquire about the learning taking place in their own classrooms and their own disciplines" (Cross and Steadman, 1996, p. 26).

Paulsen (2001), agreeing largely with Cross, notes that the capacity to conduct classroom research is a necessary condition for the scholarship of teaching. Classroom research is no longer confused with classroom assessment. The new conceptualization of classroom research presents it as a form of research "grounded in, well informed by, and interdependent with, the existing knowledge base of traditional theory and research on teaching and learning" (Paulsen, 2001, p. 9). This new conceptualization of classroom research is sufficient to constitute an act of the scholarship of teaching.

Distinctions Among Teaching Effectiveness, Scholarly Teaching, and the Scholarship of Teaching

According to Hutchings and Shulman (1999), notions about the scholarship of teaching "have evolved since its initial appearance in work by Ernest Boyer and Eugene Rice at the beginning of [the 1990s]" (p. 12). They confirm that Boyer did not "draw a sharp line between excellent teaching and the scholarship of teaching" (p. 13). In fact, they note that Boyer recognized that excellent teaching is characterized by the same mental habits that typify other types of scholarly work. Teaching is difficult work that requires considerable thought in selecting, organizing, and transforming the knowledge in one's discipline so that students can clearly understand it at a deep level. Based on this argument, a faculty member's courses are considered acts of intellectual invention and just as scholarly as a research project (Hutchings and Shulman, 1999).

Hutchings and Shulman note that the scholarship of teaching has been used as a term of approbation and has largely functioned as a way to say that good teaching matters, is serious intellectual work, and should be appropriately rewarded. In fact, they believe that all faculty have a fundamental obligation to teach well, to engage students, and to foster student learning. These minimum requirements are foundational to effective teaching. They go one step further, however, in distinguishing scholarly teaching from teaching effectiveness. When teaching "entails certain practices of classroom assessment and evidence gathering, when it is informed not by the latest ideas in the field but by current ideas about teaching the field, when it invites peer collaboration and review, then that teaching might rightly be called 'scholarly'" (p. 13).

One huge step beyond scholarly teaching is the scholarship of teaching. Three additional features must be present to be considered scholarship. Shulman and Hutchings believe that for an activity to be designated scholarship "it should be public, susceptible to critical review and evaluation, and accessible for exchange and use by other members of one's scholarly community" (1998, p. 9). A fourth attribute was later added; it involves asking questions, inquiry, and investigation around issues of student learning. For most academics, however, teaching is a private act, rarely evaluated by colleagues, where innovative teaching initiatives are not built on the work of others and are not shared with the academy.

Clearly through the eyes of Hutchings and Shulman, the scholarship of teaching is not synonymous with scholarly teaching or teaching effectiveness. Instead, the scholarship of teaching is a process through which the profession of teaching itself advances. It occurs when faculty systematically investigate questions related to student learning, and it happens with one eye on improving their own classroom performance and the other on advancing the practice. The scholarship of teaching requires "going meta" and investigating the conditions under which students learn. How does learning occur? What does it look like? How can it be deepened? (Hutchings and Shulman, 1999).

Hutchings and Shulman believe that one important step in advancing the scholarship of teaching is to develop teaching academies across the country that can serve as support centers, sanctuaries, and learning centers for scholars across disciplines pursuing the scholarship of teaching. Through the support of The Pew Foundation and the Carnegie Foundation for the Advancement of Teaching, these Carnegie Teaching Academies have already started to develop. In fact, the Carnegie Teaching Academy has drafted a definition of the scholarship of teaching as a starting point to begin campus conversations across the country. According to the Carnegie Teaching Academy, "the scholarship of teaching is problem posing about an issue of teaching or learning, study of the problem through methods appropriate to disciplinary epistemologies, application of results to practice, communication of results, self-reflection, and peer review" (Hutchings, 1999, p. 7).

A Narrower View of the Scholarship of Teaching

In fact, Richlin (2001) takes an even narrower approach to the scholarship of teaching than Hutchings and Shulman. She believes the scholarship of teaching has gotten confused with the act of teaching itself. Richlin attributes part of this confusion to Glassick, Huber, and Maeroff's *Scholarship Assessed: Evaluation of the Professoriate* (1997). Richlin notes that in *Scholarship Assessed,* the authors use a different process for evaluating teaching from that used for the other three domains. Instead of using criteria used by journals and conferences to select their articles and presentations, Richlin points out that the process of teaching was evaluated through the review of teaching evaluation documents from campuses.

Although Richlin concedes that scholarly teaching and the scholarship of teaching are closely related, she believes they differ in their intent and their product. "The purpose of scholarly teaching is to impact the activity of teaching and the resulting learning, while the scholarship of teaching results in a formal, peer-reviewed communication in appropriate media or venue, which then becomes part of the Knowledge Base of Teaching and Learning in Higher Education" (2001, p. 2).

Richlin believes that the scholarly process requires two elements—the systematic observation of the teaching-learning connection and contextualizing the results of a teaching intervention. The first element is what Richlin considers scholarly teaching. It becomes the scholarship of teaching only when this scholarly investigation leads to a manuscript to be "submitted to an appropriate journal or conference venue" (2001, p. 4). According to Richlin, the scholarship of teaching can be read in the higher education pedagogical journals just like any other disciplinary form of scholarship. There is absolutely no confusion in her mind between teaching effectiveness, scholarly teaching, and the scholarship of teaching.

Seeking Agreement on the Scholarship of Teaching

Kreber (2001a) has taken a slightly different approach to the scholarship of teaching. Acknowledging that considerable confusion remains regarding the meaning of the scholarship of teaching, she believes it will be difficult to assess the scholarship of teaching until some agreement can be reached on a definition. To attempt to reach such an agreement, Kreber gathered a panel of eleven experts in this area and asked two open-ended questions: What are the key features or components of the scholarship of teaching? What issues surrounding the scholarship of teaching are still unresolved (2001a)? Interestingly, the panel agreed on more unresolved issues than on various components of the scholarship of teaching. Using the delphi method, the experts were able to achieve some level of consensus on eighteen statements, among them:

> Those [who] practice the scholarship of teaching carefully design ways to examine, interpret, and share learning about teaching. Faculty [who] practice the scholarship of teaching are curious about the ways in which students learn and the effects of certain practices on that learning. . . .

> The scholarship of teaching has characteristics that make it different from other forms of scholarship, but it also has characteristics that encompass the dimensions of the scholarship of discovery, integration, and application.

> Engaging in classroom research is important but is not sufficient for the scholarship of teaching. . . . [p. 14]

In another article, Kreber discusses how the scholarship of teaching might become built into our graduate programs and faculty development initiatives.

She is perplexed that our graduate programs claim to educate future academics in the disciplines as related to advancing and disseminating knowledge but that teaching, the most widely used way to disseminate knowledge, receives no attention (Kreber, 2001b).

Kreber notes that sixteen of the twenty-one agreed-upon unresolved issues suggest that "the scholarship of teaching is driven by a desire to understand how students learn and how to teach more effectively, requires a theoretical framework, involves reflection and the development of pedagogical content knowledge and overlaps with other aspects of scholarship" (2001b, p. 18). The key point in Kreber's study is that "the scholarship of teaching can be shared and demonstrated not only through peer-reviewed publications or conference proposals, but also by peer-reviewed learning processes" (2001b, p. 19). Among the processes Kreber mentions are teaching a class and videotaping it to assess the effectiveness on instructional strategies or participating in a debate and discussing the relative merits of large-group versus small-group teaching.

Assessing the Scholarship of Teaching

Centra (2001) believes that the scholarship of teaching can be assessed on three levels and three dimensions. The levels of the scholarship of teaching are the individual teacher, the department, and the institution. The three dimensions of the scholarship of teaching include making teaching public, focusing on teaching practices and learning outcomes, and having content and pedagogical knowledge.

The first dimension, making teaching public, "is a combination of being open about one's teaching and being instructive to others" (Centra, 2001, p. 2). It includes academics' sharing their learning about teaching as well as opening up classrooms so that teaching can be peer reviewed and useful to others. The second dimension, focusing on teaching practices and learning outcomes, emphasizes "a concern about the ways in which students learn and the relation between teaching methods and learning" (p. 2). It includes understanding that students learn in diverse ways and thus must be taught in diverse ways. It also focuses on investigating the relationship between teaching and learning. Centra's third dimension, having content and pedagogical knowledge, focuses on knowing one's field and how to make learning connections with students.

Centra (2001) took the three dimensions of the scholarship of teaching and the three levels of its assessment and produced a framework with nine boxes. He then developed examples of possible practices and criteria for each of the nine boxes, resulting in fifty-three practices and policies that institutions can use to assess the scholarship of teaching at three levels.

In summary, the literature on the scholarship of teaching has dramatically expanded since the notion was first popularized in 1990. Although the expanding literature on the subject continues to advance a clearer understanding of the nature and meaning of the scholarship of teaching, it becomes increasingly distant from the concept once proposed by Boyer and Rice. It now appears to be clear that, to be considered the scholarship of teaching, some form of peer review must take place. The only argument remaining to be settled is whether the peer review process is limited to manuscripts submitted to an appropriate pedagogical higher education journal or conference. Or will the academy loosen its stranglehold on this theoretical scholarship of teaching to allow other practical peer review scholarly processes to also be included?

> **It now appears to be clear that, to be considered the scholarship of teaching, some form of peer review must take place.**

Appendix B lists forms of scholarship that reflect the objectives of the scholarship of teaching.

The Function of the Scholarship of Teaching in the Scholarship Action System

As previously discussed, social action systems require adequate performance by four functions: adaptation, goal attainment, pattern maintenance, and integration (Parsons and Platt, 1973). In the scholarship social action system, Paulsen and Feldman (1995) allocate the function of adaptation to the scholarship of teaching. Interaction with the external environment to acquire resources to develop and sustain the social action system is the role performed by adaptation (Parsons and Platt, 1973). Paulsen and Feldman (1995) posit that the scholarship of teaching performs the function of adaptation as the transmission of knowledge is exchanged for a steady stream of student enrollments. Students also offer a diversity of abilities and interests for use in the scholarship of teaching. Moreover, society provides support for the scholarship action system because of the contributions to teaching and learning made by faculty engaged in the scholarship of teaching.

Faculty Engagement in the Scholarship of Teaching

The introduction to this volume advances several guiding questions. We address these questions as they apply to the scholarship of teaching using findings from our national study of faculty (Appendix A). We use the three scholarly forms described in "Contemporary Perspectives on Boyer." These indices of faculty engagement in the scholarship of teaching are unpublished scholarly outcomes and publications. As previously indicated, we use unpublished scholarly outcomes as a proxy indicator of unpublished publicly observable scholarship. These indices are measured as composites of specific scholarly forms exhibited in Appendix B.

General Levels of Engagement in the Scholarship of Teaching

The level of faculty engagement in the scholarship of teaching sharply contrasts with that of general publication productivity levels. Moreover, striking contrasts occur between the two indices of performance of the scholarship of teaching. Specifically, the vast majority (74.7 percent) of faculty members register no publications associated with the domain of the scholarship of teaching during the previous three years (Appendix A, Table A.1). This level of publication inactivity unmistakably deviates from that indicated for general publication productivity, as 41 percent of faculty had never published during their academic careers (Boyer, 1990) and 43 percent had not published during the previous two years (Finkelstein, 1984).

An even more distinctive contrast emerges, however, for faculty production of unpublished scholarly outcomes oriented toward teaching, as an overwhelming proportion of faculty exhibit some level of activity in the creation of unpublished scholarly outcomes (99.4 percent) reflective of the scholarship of teaching (Appendix A, Table A.1).

Boyer's Prescriptions for Institutional Emphasis on the Scholarship of Teaching

Boyer (1990) advances expectations for faculty in liberal arts colleges to engage in the scholarship of teaching. He also suggests that some comprehensive colleges and universities should elect to emphasize the scholarship of teaching. We regard Boyer's expectations for institutional domain emphasis met if academics in more and less selective liberal arts colleges and in comprehensive colleges and universities publish more scholarship focused on teaching or produce more unpublished scholarly outcomes oriented toward the scholarship of teaching than do academics in other types of colleges and universities. We also consider Boyer's expectation attained if faculty members in more or less selective liberal arts colleges and comprehensive colleges and universities publish more teaching-oriented scholarship or produce more unpublished scholarly outcomes focused on teaching than they do publications or unpublished scholarly outcomes focused on the scholarships of application, discovery, or integration. Meeting either condition suffices.

Faculty members in more and less selective liberal arts colleges and in comprehensive colleges and universities match Boyer's expectations for an emphasis on the scholarship of teaching on the second criterion. Specifically, faculty members in both more and less selective liberal arts colleges and in comprehensive colleges and universities produce more unpublished scholarly outcomes oriented toward teaching than scholarship directed toward application or integration (Table A.3).

Mirroring Institutional Differences in General Publication Productivity

Research on institutional differences in general publication productivity indicates that academics in research and doctoral-granting universities exhibit greater levels of general publication productivity than faculty members in teaching-oriented colleges and universities (Finkelstein, 1984; Creswell, 1985; Fox, 1985). Publication productivity associated with the scholarship of teaching fails to parallel this pattern of institutional differences, however, as faculty across five types of colleges and universities differ little from one another in their level of publication productivity associated with the scholarship of teaching (Table A.2).

Academic Disciplines and Engagement in the Scholarship of Teaching

As described in the introduction to this volume, a robust body of literature indicates that academic disciplines exhibiting high levels of paradigmatic development differ in many ways from academic disciplines of low paradigmatic development (Braxton and Hargens, 1996). Such differences fail to occur in the case of faculty engagement in the scholarship of teaching, as faculty members in academic subject matter areas of high and low paradigmatic development exhibit similar levels of publication and the production of unpublished scholarly outcomes (Table A.4).

Faculty Characteristics and Engagement in the Scholarship of Teaching

Do individual faculty characteristics influence faculty engagement in the four domains of scholarship? Do individual faculty characteristics influence faculty engagement in the four domains of scholarship in the same way that they influence general publication productivity?

Gender. Gender exercises little or no influence on the production of unpublished scholarly outcomes and the generation of publications reflecting the scholarship of teaching (Table A.5). Thus, the effects of gender on faculty engagement in the scholarship of teaching fail to correspond with the findings of research on the influence of gender on general publication productivity (Creswell, 1985; Fox, 1985; Creamer, 1998), which suggests that male academics tend to publish more than female academics. The failure of gender to exert any influence on faculty engagement in the scholarship of teaching, however, resonates with Blackburn and Lawrence's research (1995) that found gender unrelated to general faculty publication productivity.

Race/Ethnicity. Creamer (1998) concludes from her review of research that race does not predict general publication productivity (p. 19). Her conclusion finds reinforcement in the case of engagement in the scholarship of teaching, as being Caucasian, African American, or Asian fails to influence both production of unpublished scholarly outcomes and publication productivity reflective of the scholarship of teaching (Table A.5).

Prestige of Doctoral Program. Prestige of a faculty member's doctoral program affects neither the publication of scholarship focused on teaching nor the production of scholarly outcomes directed toward teaching (Table A.5). Consequently, Fox's conclusion (1985) that prestige of the doctoral program directly or indirectly affects general publication productivity receives no backing in the case of the scholarship of teaching.

Tenure. From his review of research, Creswell (1985) concluded that tenure wields little or no effect on general publication productivity. His conclusion receives affirmation in the case of the scholarship of teaching, as holding tenure exerts little or no influence on production of scholarly outcomes and publications reflecting the scholarship of teaching (Table A.5).

Professional Age. Fox (1985) contends that educational policy should not be based on the influence of age on general publication productivity. Her contention springs from her review of research on sources of influence on general publication productivity. Her view receives partial affirmation, as professional age exercises little or no influence on faculty publication productivity within the scholarship of teaching (Table A.5). Professional age negatively influences faculty accomplishment of unpublished scholarly outcomes oriented toward teaching, however (Table A.5).

Factors Affecting the Institutionalization of a Broader Definition of Scholarship

COLLEGES AND UNIVERSITIES are bastions of change, with faculty members at the forefront of original research and innovative thinking. Yet it is somewhat of a paradox that change is a slow process at the majority of educational institutions, and many innovative programs may actually never become part of an institution's daily life. If something does happen to achieve staying power, many believe it is because it has become institutionalized.

As indicated in the introduction to this volume, institutionalization occurs at three levels: structural, procedural, and incorporation. Certain factors inherent in academic work are facilitators or barriers to the achievement of one or more of these levels of institutionalization.

Factors Affecting Structural Level Institutionalization

The use of higher education institutions as state instruments of economic development, university-industry collaboration on research, and the processes used to assess faculty scholarship play a role in structural level institutionalization of Boyer's domains of scholarship apart from discovery. State level economic development efforts and university-industry research collaboration provide some faculty members with opportunities to engage in scholarship oriented toward application. Such opportunities also develop institutional and faculty expectations for scholarship. Because such opportunities are limited, partial structural level institutionalization occurs because of these two factors.

The prevailing processes used to assess faculty scholarship performance pose a significant barrier to structural level institutionalization, however, as these processes fail to acknowledge the forms of scholarship reflecting the domains of scholarship other than discovery. Put differently, the measurement of scholarship reflecting these domains falls outside the parameters of the traditional approach to assessing faculty scholarship.

Economic Development

Hines (1988) identifies education and economic development as an important state policy issue. High-tech research centers, research parks, and incubators for small businesses in their initial stages of development are approaches to linking higher education with a state's economic development (Tucker, 1986, Zumeta, 1987). These approaches serve as a medium for the transmittal of university-based research to private industry and entrepreneurs. Findings derived from applied research are the most likely type of research findings transmitted. Applied research, which is directed toward the solution of practical problems, constitutes one aspect of the scholarship of application. College and university faculty can play a role in the communication of such findings through the production of scholarship that is unpublished but publicly observable. Examples of such forms of scholarship include the development of an innovative technology and seminars conducted for leaders of industry on applied research findings.

At first glance, state level economic development initiatives appear to facilitate the institutionalization of the scholarship of application. Hines (1988) asserts, however, that leading research and doctoral-granting universities are most likely to benefit from such initiatives. Thus, state economic development activities serve to further the engagement in the scholarship of application by faculty in research and doctoral-granting universities. Such activities, however, neither facilitate nor hinder the institutionalization of the scholarship of application in comprehensive universities and colleges. Under some circumstances, such state economic development efforts might facilitate comprehensive university and college faculty engagement in the scholarship of application. Comprehensive universities and college faculty might benefit in states undergoing economic decline, as leading research universities might lose status and resources (Slaughter and Silva, 1985).

University-Industry Research Collaboration

The 1980s witnessed the burgeoning of university-industry collaborations (Fairweather, 1988), which continued into the 1990s (Slaughter and Leslie, 1997). Such collaborations have implications for faculty engagement in the scholarship of application. Formal collaborative research agreements between industry and universities concentrate on applied research projects (Fairweather, 1988). Such agreements may result in faculty publications reporting research findings that are directly applicable to a practical problem or describing a new research problem identified through research conducted for industry. Publications of this sort reflect the scholarship of application. Other agreements between industry and universities entail the transfer of knowledge from faculty to personnel in industry and giving technical assistance (Fairweather, 1988). Publications, scholarly activities, and the production of unpublished but publicly observable scholarship indicative of the scholarship of application might result from such agreements. Articles describing the application of disciplinary knowledge and skill to a problem in industry, the development of an innovative technology, and seminars conducted for industrial staff on applied research findings are examples of such scholarship.

Collaboration between industry and universities can hinder faculty engagement in the scholarship of application if research arrangements between industry and college and university faculty restrict publication of findings. Blumenthal, Epstein, and Maxwell (1986) report that such restrictions include delays in publication of research results and the prohibition of the publication of research results. Restrictions of this type greatly hinder the institutionalization of the scholarship of application, as faculty publication productivity suffers.

Facilitation of the institutionalization of the scholarship of application obtains primarily for faculty in the academic disciplines of engineering, computer science, medicine, agriculture, chemistry, and biotechnology (Blumenthal, Epstein, and Maxwell, 1986; Nelson, 1986; Peters and Fusfeld, 1983, Wofsy, 1986). Conversely, the institutionalization of the scholarship of application by faculty members in other academic disciplines is neither facilitated nor hindered by industry-university research agreements. In addition, such agreements enhance further institutionalization of the scholarship of application in research universities, given that the majority of these agreements are made with research universities (Fairweather, 1988). Research agreements with local companies (Logan and Stampen, 1985) also advance the institutionalization of the scholarship of application in comprehensive universities and colleges.

Assessment of Faculty Scholarship

The processes used to assess faculty scholarship play a complementary role in the prevailing reward structure, as assessments provide the basis for the allocation of academic rewards. This process takes the form of a traditional assessment template (Braxton and Del Favero, forthcoming), which consists of articles in refereed academic journals, book chapters, scholarly books, and monographs as the predominant forms of publications used to assess faculty scholarship performance. Straight counts of these publication forms provide a quantitative appraisal of scholarship, whereas qualitative judgments involve the use of citations to published works and the quality of the refereed journal.

Braxton and Del Favero (forthcoming) contend that the suitability of using the traditional scholarship assessment template to appraise faculty performance in the scholarship domain varies across the four domains. Although they assert that the traditional template best fits the appraisal of the scholarship of discovery, they question the suitability of this template for assessing performance reflecting the scholarship of application, the scholarship of integration, and the scholarship of teaching. Their concerns revolve around the availability of publication outlets in an academic discipline and use of citations to published work to appraise quality. Low citation rates for publications associated with scholarship reflecting application, integration, and teaching minimize their value in the appraisal of scholarship quality. Aside from these important concerns, the use of scholarly activities and unpublished publicly observable scholarship to assess scholarship performance falls outside the boundaries of the traditional scholarship assessment template. This last concern is particularly problematic.

The use of the traditional scholarship assessment template hinders the institutionalization of the scholarship of application, the scholarship of integration, and the scholarship of teaching. The traditional assessment template also thwarts Boyer's call to align the academic reward structure to account for the day-to-day scholarly activities of faculty members and to correspond to the institutional mission of collegiate institutions other than the research university.

Factors Affecting Procedural Level Institutionalization

Faculty workload patterns reflect standard institutional policies about the division of faculty work among research, service, and teaching. As previously stated, procedural level institutionalization occurs when the object of institutionalization becomes a part of the standard operating procedures of a college or university. Consequently, prevailing faculty workload patterns play a significant part in procedural level institutionalization.

Faculty across all types of colleges and universities, with the exception of public two-year colleges, work in excess of fifty hours per week (Meyer, 1998). Academics in four-year colleges and universities work an average of nearly 55 hours per week (Fairweather, 1996). Given such a time commitment, upward limits exist on expanding the professional obligations of faculty.

Moreover, teaching is a contractual obligation to the institution for most college and university faculty members. Teaching loads remain fixed for faculty at teaching-oriented colleges and universities, whereas faculty in research and doctoral-granting universities may reduce their teaching loads through research grants and course buyouts (Massy and Zemsky, 1994). These factors, plus the considerable amount of time faculty commit to teaching across the full range of colleges and universities, strongly indicate that the capacity for greater levels of faculty engagement in the four domains of scholarship is structurally limited across different types of colleges and universities. Faculty members in research universities hold the most discretionary time, allocating an average of 42.6 percent of their time to teaching (Fairweather, 1996). Academics in doctoral-granting universities, who allocate 53.7 percent of their time to teaching (Fairweather, 1996), possess more discretionary time than their counterparts in comprehensive universities and colleges and in liberal arts colleges. Moreover, Milem, Berger, and Dey (2000) report that the time faculty devote to teaching has increased since 1972.

In stark contrast, faculty in comprehensive universities and colleges and liberal arts colleges possess much less discretionary time that could be devoted to scholarship. More specifically, academics in comprehensive universities and colleges allocate 63.8 percent of their time to teaching, and academics in liberal arts colleges devote 68 percent of their time to teaching (Fairweather, 1996).

Such patterns of time commitments indicate that faculty members in comprehensive universities and colleges and liberal arts colleges who seldom or never engage in any of the four domains of scholarship hold little discretionary time needed for such engagement. Hence, the time devoted to teaching impedes the realization of Boyer's prescriptions for domain emphasis in these types of colleges and universities. More specifically, Boyer's expectations for an emphasis on the scholarship of application and the scholarship of integration for faculty members in comprehensive universities and colleges and his expectations for an emphasis on the scholarship of integration by faculty members in liberal arts colleges are significantly limited.

Likewise, limits also exist on the realization of Boyer's expectations for an emphasis on the scholarship of teaching among liberal arts college faculty. Nevertheless, the vast percentage of time faculty in liberal arts colleges devote to teaching may function as a foundation, or crucible, for their engagement in various forms of scholarship reflecting this domain. From their extensive time commitment to teaching, opportunities and ideas suitable for publication or the development of unpublished but publicly observable forms of scholarship may emerge for faculty uninvolved in the scholarship of teaching.

Factors Affecting Incorporation Level Institutionalization

As indicated, incorporation level institutionalization occurs when institutional values and norms associated with the object of institutionalization are embedded in the culture of the organization. Several factors, however, represent extant patterns of values that may impede incorporation level institutionalization of Boyer's perspective on expanding the boundaries of scholarship: the academic reward structure, graduate education, and scholarly role acquisition by community college faculty members. In contrast, the value academics place on engagement in each of the four domains of scholarship suggests the possibility of incorporation level institutionalization.

Academic Reward System

The academic community highly values and allocates recognition for originality in research, or the scholarship of discovery. Publications function as the basis for scholarly recognition (Fox, 1985). Publications also serve as the primary medium for the communication of research findings to the academic community (Mullins, 1973; Fox, 1985).

As a consequence, the scholarship of discovery and publications provide the primary basis for the allocation of rewards in the academic profession. At the institutional level, these rewards include tenure, promotion, and salary. Tuckman (1976) found that increases in the number of publications increase the probability of an individual's promotion to associate professor. His findings hold across different academic disciplines and different types of colleges and universities.

Publications also significantly affect faculty salaries (Tuckman, 1976; Tuckman and Hagemann, 1976; Katz, 1973). Particularly telling is research by Fairweather (1996); he found that publications influence faculty salaries in research and doctoral-granting universities and as well as in such teaching-oriented institutions as comprehensive universities and colleges and liberal arts colleges. Fairweather (1996) points to the misalignment between institutional mission and faculty rewards in comprehensive universities and colleges and liberal arts colleges, stating that the pattern of influence of publications on salary occurs "despite the differences in professed institutional missions" (p. 61).

Thus, the prevailing academic reward structure presents a significant barrier to the institutionalization of Boyer's four domains of scholarship. The academic reward structure impedes the institutionalization of Boyer's formulations across different types of colleges and universities. It is particularly problematic, however, for the institutionalization of those domains of scholarship considered by Boyer to be congruent with the institutional missions of liberal arts colleges and comprehensive universities and colleges. Specifically, the predominant academic reward structure impedes the institutionalization of the scholarship of application in comprehensive universities and colleges, the institutionalization of the scholarship of integration in liberal arts colleges and in comprehensive universities and colleges, and the institutionalization of the scholarship of teaching in liberal arts colleges.

Graduate Education

Graduate education at the doctoral level functions as a powerful socialization process (Hagstrom, 1965). Doctoral students acquire knowledge, skills, competencies, norms, attitudes, and values important for professional role performance through this process (Merton, Reader, and Kendall, 1957). For the academic disciplines, this socialization process inculcates attitudes, values, norms, and skills for performance of the research role (Hagstrom, 1965; Cole and Cole, 1973). Put differently, perspectives on the scholarly role, work styles, and standards of role performance are shaped by doctoral education (Zuckerman, 1977). This socialization process encompasses the total context of graduate education (Toombs, 1977), consisting of such formal dimensions as courses, qualifying examinations, and the dissertation. This process also entails such informal dimensions as faculty-student interpersonal interactions and exchanges with the ambient environment (Toombs, 1977). Moreover, the effects of doctoral socialization endure throughout the academic career (Kuhn, 1970; Mullins, 1973).

The powerful and enduring effects of graduate education raise a question about whether such socialization predisposes faculty members toward engaging in the scholarship of application, discovery, integration, or teaching. The types of doctoral dissertations supported by doctoral-granting universities provide one approach to assessing the role graduate education plays in shaping faculty predispositions toward these domains of scholarship. Richlin (1993) provides such evidence from her research on the types of doctoral dissertations likely to be awarded by research and doctoral-granting universities. She reports that the scholarship of discovery receives almost full support, whereas the scholarship of teaching receives the least amount of support, as slightly more than a third (33.4 percent) of such institutions indicate they would be likely to award a Ph.D. for a dissertation focusing on the scholarship of teaching. The scholarship of integration receives considerable support, as almost two-thirds of deans and department chairs indicate they would award a Ph.D. for dissertations reflecting this form of scholarship. The scholarship of application receives middling support. Although Richlin includes chairs from four academic disciplines representing high (biology and mathematics) and low (history and psychology) paradigmatic development, she does not provide findings along such disciplinary lines. Given the disciplinary differences we observe for various indices of the scholarship of integration and the scholarship of teaching, differences in the level of support for these domains of scholarship in graduate education may obtain between these disciplines of high and low paradigmatic development.

Richlin's findings (1993) suggest the following conclusions. Graduate education, for the most part, currently discourages future faculty members from pursuing the scholarship of teaching. Thus, graduate study represents a major barrier to the institutionalization of the scholarship of teaching. Moreover, graduate education functions as a modest barrier to the institutionalization of the scholarship of application. As we might expect, future faculty members appear to be strongly socialized to engage in the scholarship of discovery, followed by the scholarship of integration. Accordingly, graduate education perpetuates the preeminence of the scholarship of discovery while posing little or no threat to the institutionalization of the scholarship of integration. The last chapter of this volume provides recommendations for altering graduate education.

Graduate study represents a major barrier to the institutionalization of the scholarship of teaching.

Role Acquisition by Community College Faculty

The community college presents a special problem for the institutionalization of Boyer's expanded definition of scholarship. Teaching is a central mission of the community college. Moreover, community colleges embrace service to their communities as part of their institutional missions (Cohen and Brawer,

1982). Consequently, Boyer's expectations for the engagement of community college faculty in the scholarship of teaching and the scholarship of application correspond with the mission of the community college.

The culture of the community college fails to embrace the faculty scholarly role in the community college, however (Vaughan, 1988). Although Vaughan discusses five reasons for this failure, two reasons are particularly relevant to the institutionalization of Boyer's perspective in community colleges: the failure of community colleges to link scholarship to teaching and the failure of community colleges to reward scholarship. Vaughan contends that community colleges celebrate their role as teaching institutions but fail to recognize that effective teaching cannot occur without the benefit of scholarship. He also points out that scholarship is rarely a criterion in the promotion and tenure process in community colleges. Vaughan's assertions indicate that the acquisition of the scholarly role by community college faculty poses an obstacle to the institutionalization of the scholarships of teaching and application. Put differently, community college faculty engagement in the scholarship of these two domains depends on their internalization of the scholarly role.

Research by Palmer (1992), however, suggests more involvement in scholarship by community college faculty than expected from Vaughan's arguments. Although Boyer's four domains of scholarship did not guide Palmer's research, several categories of scholarship Palmer used correspond to the scholarship of application (e.g., research or technical reports disseminated internally to the college or to other clients, community informational materials designed for the general public or to help area businesses improve operations, and technical innovations such as a new technology for use in the operation of a business or industry) and the scholarship of teaching (e.g., instructional materials such as instructional software and unpublished textbooks or learning guides used by colleagues). Palmer's research shows that community college faculty members exhibit greater levels of performance in the scholarship of teaching than in the scholarship of application. The levels of performance range from a high of 34 percent (instructional materials) to a low of 12 percent (technical innovations) of community college faculty members producing a piece of scholarship during the previous two years.

Although community college faculty members produce more scholarship than anticipated given Vaughan's assertions, the acquisition of the scholarly role by community college faculty remains problematic as indicated by the large proportion of scholarly inactive faculty members. Thus, the acquisition or internalization of the scholarly role presents a barrier to the institutionalization of the scholarship of application and the scholarship of teaching in community colleges.

Espousal of Values Toward the Four Domains of Scholarship

Values influence behaviors (Rokeach, 1973). Accordingly, values may also influence the involvement of college and university faculty members in various forms of scholarship. Blackburn and Lawrence (1995) found empirical support for the influence of self-knowledge and social knowledge on general publication productivity of college and university faculty. Self-knowledge includes individual values, whereas social knowledge includes values held by the college or university as an organization (Blackburn and Lawrence, 1995). Fox (1985) provides additional conceptual support for the notion of social knowledge, contending that the academic setting may influence publication productivity.

Our national study of faculty performance of scholarly activities associated with Boyer's four domains of scholarship enables us to offer an indication of the values held toward the four domains of scholarship by individual faculty members (self-knowledge), department colleagues (social knowledge), and the college or university of academic appointment (social knowledge). Appendix A describes the methodology and statistical procedure used to assess these values.

As previously indicated, Boyer (1990) holds that faculty members in doctoral-granting universities and in comprehensive universities and colleges should stress the scholarship of application. He asserts the scholarship of application fits the mission of such universities and colleges. The institutionalization of the scholarship of application in comprehensive colleges and universities and in doctoral-granting universities depends to some extent on the value placed on this domain by individual faculty members, departmental colleagues, and the institution. Individual faculty members, academic

---

departments, and the institution place a high value on the scholarship of application in both doctoral-granting universities and comprehensive universities and colleges. To elaborate, more than 90 percent of faculty members in both types of collegiate institutions agree or strongly agree that they value the scholarship of application. More than 80 percent of academics in both types of colleges and universities agree or strongly agree that their college or university values the scholarship of application. Somewhat different levels of agreement obtain, however, for these two types of institutions on faculty perceptions of the value placed on this domain of scholarship by their departmental colleagues, as 79.4 percent of faculty members in comprehensive universities and colleges and 69.1 percent of academics in doctoral-granting universities agree or strongly agree that most of their departmental colleagues value the scholarship of application. Thus, the value placed on the scholarship of application by individual academics, departmental colleagues, and the college or university of academic appointment enhances the institutionalization of the scholarship of application in doctoral-granting universities and in comprehensive universities and colleges (Appendix A, Tables A.6 and A.7).

The scholarship of discovery best fits the institutional missions of the research university and to some extent the mission of the doctoral-granting university (Boyer, 1990). The value ascribed to the scholarship of discovery by individual faculty members, departmental colleagues, and the university greatly corresponds to the research mission of such universities. Accordingly, the value placed on the scholarship of discovery augments the institutionalization of the scholarship of discovery in research and doctoral-granting universities. More specifically, more than 95 percent of faculty members in both types of universities agree or strongly agree that they value the scholarship of discovery. Moreover, more than 90 percent of academics in these institutional categories agree or strongly agree that most of their departmental colleagues value the scholarship of discovery. Finally, more than 90 percent of faculty members in research and doctoral-granting universities agree or strongly agree that their universities value the scholarship of discovery (Tables A.6 and A.7).

Boyer (1990) prescribes that faculty members in liberal arts colleges and comprehensive universities and colleges emphasize the scholarship of integration. He holds that engagement in the scholarship of integration aligns with the mission of such colleges and universities. More than 90 percent of academics in liberal arts colleges–I and –II and in comprehensive universities and colleges attach a high value to the scholarship of integration. Departmental colleagues assign less value to the scholarship of application, as 60.2 percent of faculty members in comprehensive universities and colleges agree or strongly agree that most of their departmental colleagues value this scholarly domain. About 70 percent of academics in liberal arts colleges–I (70.8 percent) and liberal arts colleges–II (68.6 percent) agree or strongly agree that colleagues in their departments value the scholarship of integration. Faculty in these teaching-oriented colleges also believe that their institutions value the scholarship of integration. Specifically, 70 percent of academics in comprehensive universities and colleges, 79.5 percent in liberal arts colleges–I, and 70.7 percent in liberal arts colleges–II agree or strongly agree that their college or university values this domain. Taken together, these proportions indicate that the value placed on the scholarship of integration by individual faculty members, departmental colleagues, and the college or university of employment poses little or no barrier to the institutionalization of the scholarship of integration in liberal arts colleges and comprehensive universities and colleges (Tables A.6 and A.7).

The scholarship of teaching corresponds to the institutional missions of liberal arts colleges. Accordingly, Boyer (1990) asserts that faculty members in liberal arts colleges should stress this scholarly domain. Individual faculty members in both liberal arts colleges–I and –II highly value the scholarship of teaching as indicated by the percentage of individuals who agree or strongly agree that they value this domain of scholarship. Specifically, 83.2 percent of faculty in more selective liberal arts colleges espouse such levels of agreement, whereas 91.1 percent of their counterparts in less selective liberal arts colleges do so. More than 80 percent of academics in liberal arts colleges–II agree or strongly agree that most of their departmental colleagues and their colleges value engagement in the scholarship of teaching. Although less substantial, more than 60 percent of faculty members in more selective liberal arts colleges agree or strongly agree that most of their departmental colleagues and colleges value faculty efforts in the scholarship of teaching domain. Faculty in more and less selective liberal arts colleges also hold that their colleges place a high value on the scholarship of teaching. For more and less selective liberal arts colleges, the value attached to the scholarship of teaching by individual faculty members, departmental colleagues, and the institution present little or no obstacle to the institutionalization of the scholarship of teaching in these two types of teaching institutions (Tables A.6 and A.7).

In sum, scholarly values at the level of the individual, the department, and the institution foster the institutionalization of all four domains of scholarship along the lines of Boyer's expectations for institutional domain. Put differently, self-knowledge (individual values) and social knowledge (departmental colleagues and the institution) reinforce the value placed on engagement in the domain of scholarship that matches Boyer's perspective on the appropriate mission for a given type of college or university.

The next chapter presents various approaches to changing the academic reward structure and the assessment of faculty scholarship. We devote a separate chapter because the academic reward structure and its accompanying scholarship assessment process must be fundamentally changed to attain the incorporation level of the institutionalization of Boyer's arguments.

Approaches to Altering
the Academic Reward System

S ALARY INCREASES, TENURE, AND PROMOTION are important mechanisms for rewarding and recognizing the scholarship of faculty members. Through such decisions, deep-seated norms and values about academic work manifest themselves. As indicated in the previous chapter, the academic reward system that prevails at most colleges and universities presents a significant obstacle to the institutionalization of Boyer's four domains of scholarship. Without alterations in this system, institutional values and norms supporting Boyer's arguments are unlikely to predominate. Incorporation level institutionalization cannot occur if institutional values and norms supporting Boyer's expanded view of scholarship are not assimilated into the culture of colleges and universities so as to guide institutional action. This chapter reviews some approaches to altering the academic reward system, with particular attention to the tenure and promotion process.

Essential Attributes of Tenure and Promotion Systems

Diamond (1993, 1999) asserts that tenure and promotion systems must exhibit some essential attributes. He contends that most tenure and promotion systems fail to exhibit these characteristics. Although he describes five attributes, three of them are of particular salience to Boyer's arguments.

The first essential attribute of importance to the institutionalization of Boyer's perspective is that a tenure and promotion system must correspond to the mission of the college or university (Diamond, 1993, 1999). This attribute resonates with Boyer's contention that the prevailing academic reward system that emphasizes publication and the scholarship of discovery fails to align with the missions of most colleges and universities. If the mission of the institution is to emphasize the scholarship of teaching, then the tenure and promotion system must award tenure and promotion to faculty who engage in scholarship oriented toward this domain.

> **If the mission of the institution is to emphasize the scholarship of teaching, then the tenure and promotion system must award tenure and promotion to faculty who engage in scholarship oriented toward this domain.**

Sensitivity to differences among academic disciplines constitutes a second essential characteristic of tenure and promotion systems (Diamond, 1993, 1999). This characteristic is integral to efforts to institutionalize Boyer's expanded definition of scholarship. This attribute acknowledges the disciplinary differences in general publication productivity described in the introduction to this volume. This characteristic also takes into account our findings noting distinctions in faculty engagement in various forms of scholarship associated with the four domains of scholarship.

An assessment system that faculty members perceive as fair and workable is a third key characteristic of tenure and promotion systems (Diamond, 1993). Such a system will be perceived as fair and workable if it acknowledges scholarship conducted in each of the four domains of scholarship. It will also be viewed as fair and workable if it counts scholarship in forms apart from publications as Boyer (1990) recommends. In a subsequent section of this chapter, we describe more fully approaches to the assessment of faculty scholarship congruent with Boyer's perspective.

Administrative and Faculty Involvement

Diamond (1993) posits that changes in tenure and promotion systems require the commitment of both the administration and faculty members. Both have responsibilities in the change process.

Administrative Responsibilities

Diamond (1993) states that the president and the chief academic officer must exercise leadership for change in the tenure and promotion system. Such leadership is exercised through five imperatives for administrative action (Diamond, 1993). First, the central administration must include change in the promotion and tenure process on the agenda for institutional action. All members of the campus community must clearly understand the commitment of the central administration to change the tenure and promotion process. Thus, the president and chief academic officer of colleges and universities seeking incorporation level institutionalization of Boyer's perspective must make a commitment to align the tenure and promotion system at their college or university with Boyer's formulations.

Second, the central administration must set forth a process for making changes in the tenure and promotion system (Diamond, 1993). The central administration must assume responsibility for establishing guidelines, general procedures, and time lines for change. Such guidelines bolster the role of promotion and tenure committees and academic departments in changing the tenure and promotion system. The central administration of colleges and universities pursuing the institutionalization of Boyer's arguments should establish such a process.

The central administration must also assume responsibility for the development or revision of the institutional mission to reflect the desired changes in the tenure and promotion system (Diamond, 1993)—the third responsibility of the central administration. Mission statements establish priorities for the college or university and serve as the basis for the allocation of rewards such as tenure and promotion to faculty. Diamond (1993) recommends that the institutional mission be understood and accepted by faculty, administrators, and students.

Colleges and universities striving for incorporation level institutionalization must alter or develop their institutional mission statements to coincide with Boyer's prescriptions for emphasis on institutional scholarship. Such mission statements must clearly state the mission of the scholarship pursued by faculty at the focal college or university. To be consistent with Boyer's prescriptions for institutional domain emphasis, the central administration of comprehensive universities and colleges should foster the development of mission statements that emphasize the scholarships of application and integration. The central administration of liberal arts colleges should encourage the development of mission statements that stress the scholarship of integration and teaching. Community college presidents and chief academic officers should facilitate the development of mission statements that underscore the scholarship of teaching. The president and chief academic officer of research and doctoral-granting universities wishing to institutionalize domains of scholarship other than discovery at the incorporation level should alter their mission statements to reflect the priority the pursuit of these other domains of scholarship hold at their universities.

Fourth, the central administration must also actively involve faculty members in the process of changing the tenure and promotion system (Diamond, 1993). Diamond notes that individual faculty members and their colleagues who serve on tenure and promotion committees function as agents of change in the tenure and promotion system. Hence, the president and chief academic officer of colleges and universities pursuing incorporation level institutionalization of Boyer's formulations must also actively engage faculty in the process of changing the tenure and promotion system to correspond to Boyer's perspectives.

Diamond's fifth imperative for the central administration (1993) serves to reinforce the commitment of the president and chief academic officer to change the tenure and promotion system. He recommends the issuing of regular progress reports on the change process and that needed changes be routinely communicated in various administrative messages and communications. The central administration of colleges and universities seeking to institutionalize Boyer's arguments at the incorporation level should also exercise this imperative.

Faculty Responsibilities

Professions demand the right to assess the professional role performance of colleagues (Light, 1974; Baldridge, Curtis, Ecker, and Riley, 1978), and the academic profession is no exception. As a consequence, the faculty of a college or university committed to changing the tenure and promotion system must fully participate in the change process. Diamond's fourth imperative for administrative action recognizes this social reality. Moreover, faculty members and their colleagues who serve on tenure and promotion committees bear the major responsibility for implementing change in the tenure and promotion system.

Accordingly, Diamond (1993) recommends that each academic unit establish its own criteria for tenure and promotion. The range of scholarly activities judged appropriate must also be delineated. Both criteria and the range of appropriate scholarly activities must be specific and clearly stated (Diamond, 1993, 1999). To achieve incorporation level institutionalization of Boyer's perspective, the criteria and delineation of appropriate scholarship by academic units should match Boyer's formulations, especially those consistent with the scholarly objectives and norms of their academic discipline.

Tenure and promotion committees bear the responsibility for understanding the criteria and range of appropriate scholarly activities that academic units promulgate for tenure and promotion (Diamond, 1993). Members of tenure and promotion committees must also strive not to apply criteria and scholarship assessment procedures used in their academic discipline to faculty candidates for tenure and promotion from other academic disciplines (Diamond, 1993).

Criteria for Altering the Assessment of Scholarship

As previously demonstrated, the development of appropriate criteria for tenure and promotion constitutes an integral part of the process of changing the tenure and promotion system. Thus, the development of criteria for tenure and promotion consistent with Boyer's formulations is imperative for incorporation level institutionalization of an expansion of the boundaries of scholarship beyond the scholarship of discovery and the use of forms of scholarship other than publications to assess performance.

Two important issues for assessing scholarship along the lines of Boyer's perspectives emerge. The first issue concerns his view that forms of scholarship other than publications be used to assess faculty scholarship performance.

Basically, this issue involves the attributes academic work must possess to be judged as scholarship. The second issue revolves around the need to specify the types of scholarship that reflect faculty engagement in each of the four domains.

This subsection reviews criteria that may be used to judge whether a piece of academic work fits the parameters of scholarship.

Broad Criteria

The chapter titled "The Four Domains of Scholarship: Toward a Rethinking of Scholarly Role Performance" notes that perspectives on academic work fitting the parameters of scholarship may be placed on a continuum. This continuum differentiates scholarly activities from scholarship. At one end, Richlin (2001) holds that only academic work in the form of publications in formal, peer-reviewed journals may be judged as scholarship. If we relax this viewpoint to some extent, publications in a variety of forms (e.g., textbooks and writings for the popular press) may also be judged as scholarship.

Scholarly activities occupy the other end of the continuum. Activities performed by faculty members may be judged scholarly if disciplinary knowledge and skill are used in performing the activity (Braxton and Bayer, 1986). Many day-to-day activities of faculty fit this definition of scholarly activity.

Shulman and Hutchings's view (1998) on the essential characteristics of scholarship hold middle ground on this continuum. They outline three such characteristics: the work must be public, amenable to peer review, and in a form that allows for exchange and use by members of the academic community. Unpublished publicly observable outcomes of scholarly activity within the four domains of scholarship, if in appropriate form for exchange and peer review, meet these three essential characteristics.

Specific Criteria

Diamond (1993, 1999) and Glassick, Huber, and Maeroff (1997) advance a set of criteria that may also be used to appraise whether a piece of academic work fits the parameters of scholarship. These specific criteria may also be used to appraise the quality of a piece of academic work judged to meet the parameters of scholarship.

Diamond (1993) advances a set of six criteria commonly applied in tenure and promotion systems: the faculty member's work exhibits a high level of discipline-based expertise, breaks new ground or is innovative, can be replicated or elaborated upon by others, can be documented, can be reviewed by peers, and is significant or has impact. He asserts that these criteria define faculty work as scholarship.

Four of these criteria fit well Boyer's domains of scholarship and his mandate for forms of scholarship other than publications: the work demonstrates a high level of discipline-based expertise, can be documented, can be reviewed by peers, and is significant or has impact. The criteria of replicability and originality best fit the scholarship of discovery.

As useful as *Scholarship Reconsidered* may have been in getting academics to broaden their perception of scholarship, "the real issue revolves around how to assess other forms of scholarship" (Glassick, Huber, and Maeroff, 1997, p. 21). In other words, before teaching, integration, and application can be considered on a par with discovery, each would have to be vigorously assessed to withstand the scrutiny of being called *scholarship*. In fact, rather than detailing specific qualities for describing scholarly work for each domain, Glassick, Huber, and Maeroff focused on the process of scholarship and sought commonalities that might be present in any scholarly work.

In an effort to shape the debate and bring focus to this issue, Glassick, Huber, and Maeroff propose six criteria to assess the quality of scholarship in the four domains (1997). According to the authors, scholarship in all of its forms involves a common sequence of unfolding stages. They say the following six criteria must be present before any work might rightly be considered scholarship: clear goals, adequate preparation, appropriate methods, significant results, effective presentation, and reflective critique.

Clear Goals. The first step in the common sequence of unfolding stages involves clear goals. Has the basic question or purpose been clearly stated? Have the objectives been defined, and are they realistic and achievable? Did the professor clearly state the objectives of the course, and were the proposed objectives actually taught?

Adequate Preparation. If the first hurdle is met, one of the most basic aspects of scholarly work is adequate preparation. Does the scholarship appear current, and does it reflect an understanding of the existing work in the field? Does the scholar possess the necessary skills and bring together the resources required to move the project forward? Fundamentally, the depth and breadth of the scholar's understanding of the subject matter—the mastery of certain necessary skills—determine the quality of scholarly work. Glassick, Huber, and Maeroff believe that any scholarship—discovery, integration, application, or teaching—must demonstrate adequate preparation.

Appropriate Methods. The third of the six criteria essential for scholarly work is appropriate methods. The methods must be chosen wisely, applied effectively, and modified judiciously as a project evolves. The methodology must be elegantly designed to give the project integrity and the audience confidence. In assessing teaching as a scholarly work, one might ask whether the methods of evaluating a student's work were fair and effective. Was the course presented in logical sequence, and was the amount of material the instructor attempted to cover appropriate? Finally, a scholar needs to be a good craftsman, modifying procedures and responding flexibly to changing circumstances.

Significant Results. According to Glassick, Huber, and Maeroff (1997), "any act of scholarship must also be judged by the significance of its results" (p. 29). Does the work add consequentially to the field of knowledge? Does it make a significant contribution to the literature? Did the teacher stimulate the student's interest in the subject matter being taught? Have new areas of exploration been opened up through the scholar's work, and have the goals for the project been achieved? All of these questions are appropriate in determining the significance of the scholarly work.

Effective Presentation. The most significant results are not scholarly if they are not presented effectively. The work must be effectively organized and presented in a suitable style with clarity and integrity. Is the manuscript well written? Is the writing style effective? Did the teacher communicate clearly?

Effective presentation includes a sense of audience and figuring out how to communicate most effectively with its members. Is the audience tracking the presentation in written form or even the spoken word?

Reflective Critique. The final stage in any scholarly work involves reflective critique. The scholar should critically evaluate his or her own work to improve the quality of future work. Through learning from this process and the opinions of others, the scholar can seek ways to improve the process of scholarship itself.

Of these six criteria, the criterion of adequate preparation and the criterion of significant results correspond to the criteria advanced by Diamond. The criterion of adequate preparation corresponds to Diamond's requirement that a high level of discipline-based expertise be demonstrated. The criterion of significant results matches the criterion of significance or impact posited by Diamond. Taken together, Diamond's criteria and the six criteria advanced by Glassick, Huber, and Maeroff provide a strong conceptual framework for understanding and assessing the scholarships of discovery, integration, application, and teaching.

Specification of Forms of Scholarship for the Four Domains

Although Boyer (1990) provided some examples of scholarly forms reflecting the objectives of some domains of scholarship, all three levels of institutionalization—structural, procedural, and incorporation—of Boyer's perspectives will not transpire if a concrete specification of forms of scholarship oriented toward each of the four domains fails to occur. Without such a concrete specification, the measurement of faculty engagement in each of the four domains of scholarship is problematic.

Accordingly, Appendix B exhibits specific scholarly forms that reflect an orientation toward the objectives of each domain of scholarship. The inventory is organized by domain of scholarship: application, discovery, integration, and teaching. For each domain, these scholarly forms are sorted into three categories: scholarly activities, unpublished scholarly outcomes, and publications. The activities displayed under the category of unpublished scholarly outcomes meet the designation of unpublished publicly observable scholarship if the three criteria of scholarship described by Shulman and Hutchings (1998) are met. The following subsection delineates the form such activities must take for them to be labeled *scholarship*. In the inventory, however, we present these activities as possibilities. The work of Braxton and Toombs (1982), Pellino, Blackburn, and Boberg (1984), and Sundre (1992) and the examples provided by Boyer (1990) provide the foundation for the delineation of these scholarly forms.

The inventory of scholarship is a much needed step toward the measurement of faculty engagement in each of the four domains of scholarship.

The traditional scholarship assessment template best fits the scholarship of discovery (Braxton and Del Favero, forthcoming). The components of this traditional template are articles published in refereed journals, book chapters, scholarly books, and number of citations to assess quality. Academic work or academic activities not appearing in published form require the use of a new organizing template for scholarship assessment, however, Braxton and Del Favero (forthcoming) describe the requirements of this new assessment template. The requirements they set forth put unpublished pieces of academic work in a form that matches the three essential characteristics of scholarship advanced by Shulman and Hutchings (1998): the work must be public, suitable for peer review, and in a form that allows for exchange and use by peers and the lay public.

The first requirement stipulates that pieces of unpublished academic work submitted as evidence of performance in the domains of application, integration, and teaching be put in a form suitable for peer observation. Papers, presentations, reports, videos, computer software, and Web sites are examples (Braxton and Del Favero, forthcoming). Presentations must be videotaped or tape-recorded to render them publicly observable.

Documentation must accompany pieces of unpublished academic work that is publicly observable by peers, the second requirement proposed by Braxton and Del Favero (forthcoming). This requirement corresponds to a similar recommendation for documentation made by Boyer (1990), Lynton (1995), Diamond (1993), and Glassick, Huber, and Maeroff (1997).

Put differently, this requirement calls for the development of portfolios demonstrating the scholarships of application, integration, and teaching (Glassick, Huber, and Maeroff, 1997; Froh, Gray, and Lambert, 1993). Such portfolios should include the faculty member's statement outlining the goals and contributions made by his or her scholarship, a curriculum vitae listing scholarly activities performed by the individual, and selected samples of unpublished scholarship put in a form amenable to public or peer observation (Glassick, Huber, and Maeroff, 1997; Braxton and Del Favero, forthcoming).

Faculty members maintaining that their engagement in the scholarships of application, integration, or teaching springs from the type of action research described by Schön (1995) present a special case for the development of such portfolios. In their statement of goals and contributions, such faculty candidates should clearly indicate that action research constitutes the epistemological base of their scholarship. Reappointment, tenure, and promotion committees will need to identify faculty peers capable of assessing scholarship derived from action research. This recommendation stems from Schön's view (1995) that the review of scholarship derived from action research requires peers capable of assessing such scholarship.

An Initial Recommendation

This chapter outlines approaches to altering the tenure and promotion system and the scholarship assessment process. We recommend that colleges and universities serious about seeking incorporation level institutionalization of Boyer's perspective use these approaches as a foundation for institutional action. The development of institutional missions that stress institutionally appropriate objectives for faculty scholarship, however, must serve as the organizing framework for any fundamental changes in institutional academic reward systems and the concomitant scholarship assessment process. Such academic reward systems must align themselves with the objectives of faculty scholarship clearly expressed in institutional mission statements. Such mission statements should in turn reflect Boyer's prescriptions for domain emphasis by institutional type.

Conclusions and Recommendations for Further Study and for Institutional Policy and Practice

THIS CHAPTER SUMMARIZES findings from our study of faculty professional performance described in "The Scholarship of Application," "The Scholarship of Discovery," "The Scholarship of Integration," and "The Scholarship of Teaching." It also discusses the relationship of these findings to the literature on faculty scholarly role performance, advances five conclusions derived from our findings and the literature presented in this volume, and offers eleven recommendations for institutional policy and practice. These recommendations are designed to facilitate the institutionalization of Boyer's arguments into the academic work of college and university faculty members. The chapter also offers some suggestions for further research.

Summary and Discussion of Findings

This section summarizes the findings of our faculty professional performance study in relationship to each of the five research questions advanced in the introduction to this volume. The summary concentrates on publications and unpublished scholarly outcomes as indicators of faculty engagement in the four domains of scholarship. It excludes scholarly activities because we endorse the distinction between scholarly activities and scholarship made in this volume. Findings are organized according to the five research questions.

Do faculty levels of engagement in Boyer's four domains of scholarship resemble the general level of publication productivity found in research? Finkelstein (1984) indicates that 43 percent of faculty report no publications during a two-year period. Our findings show that faculty levels of publication performance for the scholarship of discovery (27.6 percent) and the scholarship of integration (25.9 percent) fall substantially below this two-year rate of inactivity for general publication productivity. In contrast, faculty levels of publication inactivity for the scholarship of application (57.1 percent) and the scholarship of teaching (74.7 percent) exceed this two-year rate for general publication inactivity.

Considerable deviation from the general level of publication inactivity indicated by Finkelstein (1984) obtains when we use unpublished scholarly outcomes as an indicator of faculty engagement in one of the four domains of scholarship. Specifically, our findings demonstrate that the vast majority of faculty produced some unpublished scholarly outcomes oriented toward the scholarship of application (74.5 percent), the scholarship of integration (65.3 percent), and the scholarship of teaching (99.4 percent).

Do faculty levels of engagement in Boyer's four domains of scholarship match Boyer's prescriptions for institutional domain emphasis? Boyer (1990) provides prescriptions for the emphasis different types of colleges and universities should place on faculty engagement in each of the four domains of scholarship. As previously indicated, he asserts that faculty members in doctoral-granting universities and comprehensive universities and colleges should stress the scholarship of application. He asserts that the scholarship of discovery should be the primary emphasis of faculty members in research and doctoral-granting universities. For academics in liberal arts colleges, Boyer recommends that the scholarship of integration and the scholarship of teaching should receive the greatest emphasis. He contends that academics in comprehensive universities and colleges should also emphasize the scholarships of integration and teaching. Our configuration of findings shows that the match between Boyer's prescriptions for institutional domain emphasis and faculty domain performance varies across the four domains.

Faculty engagement in the scholarship of discovery and the scholarship of teaching parallel Boyer's prescriptions for institutional domain emphasis. Our findings also show progress toward matching Boyer's prescriptions for institutional emphasis on the scholarships of application and integration. Nevertheless, across all five types of colleges and universities represented in our study, faculty members publish more discovery-oriented scholarship than they do scholarship focused on application, integration, and teaching.

Does faculty publication productivity in Boyer's four domains of scholarship across different types of colleges and universities mirror the level of general publication productivity exhibited across different types of colleges and universities? Research demonstrates that academics in research and doctoral-granting universities exhibit higher levels of general publication productivity than do their faculty counterparts at teaching-oriented colleges and universities (Fulton and Trow, 1974; Finkelstein, 1984; Creswell, 1985; Blackburn and Lawrence, 1995). Findings from our faculty professional performance study indicate that faculty publication productivity associated with three of the four domains of scholarship mirrors the pattern of institutional differences in general publication productivity. Specifically, faculty members in research and doctoral-granting universities publish more scholarship oriented toward the domains of application, discovery, and integration than do their academic colleagues in comprehensive universities and colleges and in more and less selective liberal arts colleges. Only faculty publication productivity in the scholarship of teaching domain fails to parallel this pattern.

Do faculty levels of engagement in Boyer's four domains of scholarship vary across different academic disciplines? As discussed in the introduction to this volume, academic disciplines vary in their level of consensus (Lodahl and Gordon, 1972; Biglan, 1973). Biology and chemistry are examples of high consensus disciplines, history and sociology of low consensus ones. Braxton and Hargens (1996) conclude from an extensive review of empirical research that faculty in high consensus fields are more oriented toward research than faculty in low consensus fields. Hence, the level of faculty engagement in the four domains of scholarship may differ between high consensus (biology and chemistry) and low consensus (history and sociology) academic disciplines.

For the scholarship of discovery and the scholarship of teaching, our findings show no differences in the level of faculty engagement among the four academic disciplines. Our findings demonstrate differences, however, among the four academic disciplines for both publications and the production of unpublished scholarly outcomes in the scholarship of application and the scholarship of integration. For the scholarship of integration, academic sociologists and academic historians exhibit higher publication levels than do their faculty colleagues in biology and chemistry. Thus, the pattern of differences between high and low consensus disciplines noted by Braxton and Hargens (1996) obtains for the scholarship of integration.

We also note disciplinary differences in the level of faculty engagement in the scholarship of application. These differences, however, are not between high and low consensus academic subject matter areas. To elaborate, academic chemists publish more application-oriented scholarship than do faculty members holding membership in the disciplines of biology, history, and sociology. In contrast, sociology faculty members produce more application-focused unpublished scholarly outcomes than do their colleagues in the disciplines of biology, chemistry, and history.

Do individual faculty characteristics influence faculty engagement in the four domains of scholarship? Do individual faculty characteristics influence faculty engagement in the four domains of scholarship in the same way that they influence general publication productivity? We organize the findings addressing this question by faculty characteristics.

• *Gender.* Our findings show that academic men tend to publish more within three of the four domains of scholarship (application, discovery, and integration) than do women academics. Men and women faculty members, however, display similar levels in the production of unpublished scholarly outcomes reflecting application and integration. Similar levels of engagement between men and women also obtain for publications and the production of unpublished scholarly outcomes in the scholarship of teaching domain. With the exception of the scholarship of teaching-, application-, and integration-oriented unpublished scholarly outcomes, the gender differences in domain engagement we observe resonate with the conclusions of scholars who have reviewed studies reporting the effects of gender on publication productivity (Creswell, 1985; Fox, 1985; Creamer, 1998).

• *Race/Ethnicity.* Race or ethnicity exerts little or no influence on faculty engagement in three of the four domains of scholarship (application, discovery, and teaching). Although we found similar levels of publication oriented toward integration, African American academics tend to produce more integration-focused unpublished scholarly outcomes than do their Caucasian or Asian faculty counterparts.

With one exception, these findings correspond to Blackburn and Lawrence's research results (1995) and with Creamer's conclusion that race does not predict publication productivity (1998, p. 19).

• *Prestige of Doctoral Program.* The prestige of a faculty member's doctoral program wields little or no influence on publication productivity associated with three of the four domains of scholarship: application, integration, and teaching. Prestige of doctoral program also wields little or no influence on the accomplishment of unpublished scholarly outcomes focused on integration. This configuration of findings fails to correspond to Fox's observation (1985), from her review of research, that prestige of doctoral program either directly or indirectly influences general publication productivity.

Nevertheless, Fox's observation receives backing from our findings for the scholarship of discovery and the production of unpublished scholarly outcomes focused on application. Specifically, the prestige of the doctoral program exerts a slight positive influence on publication productivity associated with the scholarship of discovery. Prestige of doctoral program, however, wields a slight negative influence on the production of unpublished scholarly outcomes focused on application.

• *Tenure.* Creswell (1985) concluded from his review of research on the correlates of publication productivity that tenure wields little or no influence on general publication performance. Our findings bolster his conclusion for the scholarships of application, integration, and teaching, as holding tenure exercises little or no influence on both publications and the production of unpublished scholarly outcomes associated with these three domains. Contrary to Creswell's conclusion, tenure positively affects faculty publication productivity focused on discovery.

• *Professional Age.* Finkelstein (1984) concludes from his review of research that publication productivity decreases with age, whereas Fox (1985) asserts from her review that age and productivity are weakly related at best. Creswell (1985) echoes Fox's assessment.

Our findings resonate with Finkelstein's conclusion in two ways. First, professional age negatively influences publication productivity within the domains of the scholarship of application and the scholarship of discovery. Professional age also negatively affects the production of unpublished scholarly outcomes focused on teaching.

Fox's perspective also receives support. Professional age exerts little or no influence on either measure of faculty engagement in the scholarship of integration. Publication productivity in the scholarship of teaching is also unaffected by professional age. Likewise, professional age wields little or no influence on faculty production of unpublished scholarly outcomes directed toward application.

Conclusions

We advance five conclusions derived from the findings summarized in this chapter and presented elsewhere in this volume. These conclusions are tempered, however, by the limitations of our study described in Appendix A.

The attainment of a basic knowledge of behaviors connected with the object of institutionalization constitutes structural level institutionalization (Curry, 1991). As stated in the introduction to this volume, general levels of faculty engagement offer an index of the extent of structural level institutionalization of each of the four domains of scholarship. We use both publications and unpublished scholarly outcomes as indicators of general faculty engagement in each of the four domains. Using publications as an index, structural level institutionalization exists of the scholarship of discovery and the scholarship of integration. Through the application of unpublished scholarly outcomes, evidence also results for structural level institutionalization of the scholarships of application and teaching. Thus, we conclude that all four domains of scholarship have attained structural level institutionalization.

Boyer (1990) indicates that faculty across the spectrum of colleges and university can engage in academic work in all four domains of scholarship.

He urges, however, that the academic work of faculty become better aligned with the missions of different colleges and universities. As a consequence, he developed prescriptions for the type of scholarship faculty members in different types of colleges and universities should emphasize. Given that procedural level institutionalization occurs when the behaviors and policies associated with the object of institutionalization become standard operating procedures of a college or university (Curry, 1991), as stated in the introduction to this volume, we use the extent to which faculty stress the domain of scholarship prescribed by Boyer for their type of college or university as an index of this level of institutionalization. If faculty members follow Boyer's prescriptions for institutional domain emphasis, then we can assume that the scholarly efforts of faculty have become a part of the standard operating procedures of different types of colleges or universities. Our configuration of findings suggests the conclusion that the scholarships of discovery and teaching have attained procedural level institutionalization, whereas the scholarships of application and integration show progress toward the achievement of this level of institutionalization.

The first two conclusions focus on the attainment of structural or procedural institutionalization of Boyer's arguments. This conclusion focuses on whether any of the four domains have attained both the structural and procedural levels of institutionalization. Based on the first two conclusions, we assert that the scholarships of discovery and teaching have attained both structural and procedural level institutionalization.

As described in "Factors Affecting the Institutionalization of a Broader Definition of Scholarship," institutionalization at the incorporation level is the level at which norms and values supportive of the object of institutionalization become an integral part of the organization's culture (Curry, 1991). We identify the academic reward system and graduate education as significant obstacles to incorporation level institutionalization of the scholarships of application, integration, and teaching. Despite these important barriers, our study indicates that values espoused for faculty engagement in the scholarships of application, integration, and teaching match Boyer's recommendations for institutional domain emphasis. Such value espousal occurs at the levels of the individual faculty member, the academic department, and the institution. Given that values constitute one dimension of incorpora-tion level institutionalization, we conclude that the potential exists for incorporation level institutionalization of the scholarships of application, integration, and teaching if changes supporting Boyer's formulations tran-spire in graduate education and in the academic reward system and its accompanying process of scholarship assessment.

Boyer's contention that the scholarship of discovery predominates as the most legitimate and preferred type of scholarship lies at the heart of his call for the broadening of the parameters of scholarship. Despite the spate of literature and national conferences focusing on Boyer's arguments since 1990, our findings strongly indicate that the scholarship of discovery per-sists as the most legitimate and preferred objective of faculty scholarly engagement across the spectrum of institutions of higher education.

Recommendations for Institutional Policy and Practice

Although we conclude that some aspects of Boyer's formulations have attained structural, procedural, and incorporation level institutionalization, the fol-lowing eleven recommendations are designed to further such institutionaliza-tion at these three levels. We array our recommendations according to level of institutionalization. Although each recommendation focuses on fostering a particular level of institutionalization, we contend that the implementation of each recommendation will serve to further other levels of institutionalization.

Structural Level

Assessments of faculty scholarship should use the inventory of scholarship. As pre-viously posited in this volume, the process of scholarship assessment must also change for structural and incorporation level institutionalization of Boyer's formulations to occur. We recommend that the various forms of scholarship exhibited in Appendix B provide the basis for the assessment of faculty scholarship performance for tenure and promotion decisions. We also recommend the use of both publications and unpublished scholarly out-comes contained in the inventory. In making this recommendation, we acknowledge the previously made distinction between scholarly activity and scholarship. Only scholarship, not scholarly activities, should be used in the faculty appraisal process for tenure and promotion. Unpublished scholarly outcomes, however, must meet Shulman and Hutchings's three criteria (1998) to be regarded as scholarship: the work must be public, must be suitable for peer review, and must be in an exchangeable form. For unpublished scholarly outcomes to meet these three criteria, departmental and institutional tenure and promotion committees should require that such works appear in a form that permits peer observation. Such forms include papers, audiotaped and videotaped presentations, reports, computer software, and Web sites (Braxton and Del Favero, forthcoming). Documentation along the lines suggested by various scholars (Boyer, 1990; Lynton, 1995; Diamond, 1993; Glassick, Huber, and Maeroff, 1997; Braxton and Del Favero, forthcoming) should also be required as an accompaniment to submitted unpublished scholarly outcomes that are in publicly observable form. This recommendation is consistent with Boyer's call for flexibility in the assessment of faculty scholarship.

Application and teaching scholarly activities should be used to assess faculty teaching and service performance. To bolster the demarcation between scholarly activities and scholarship, we recommend that teaching-oriented scholarly activities be used to measure faculty teaching performance for annual salary decisions and for tenure and promotion deliberations. The teaching-oriented scholarly activities displayed in Appendix B provide a means to assess the scholarly teaching of faculty members. Hutchings and Shulman (1999) differentiate scholarly teaching from teaching effectiveness, contending that faculty are obligated to teach well. Scholarly teaching, however, entails the selection, organization, and transformation of disciplinary knowledge for students' comprehension. By extension, teaching activities taking this form require the use of disciplinary knowledge and expertise in their performance. We also recommend the use of application-oriented scholarly activities to assess faculty performance of the service role (see Appendix B).

A definition of the scholarship of teaching must be embraced. Further institutionalization of the scholarship of teaching remains problematic unless agreement can be reached on the underlying objective of this domain. As stated in "The Scholarship of Teaching," much debate centers on the meaning of the scholarship of teaching. This debate creates a "conceptual quagmire" around the objectives of this domain of scholarship. Unlike the underlying objectives of the scholarships of application, discovery, and integration, the objectives of the scholarship of teaching are not clear. Accordingly, we advance a recommendation for the underlying purpose of faculty engagement in this domain of scholarship. The essence of the objective of the scholarship of teaching rests in Boyer's contention that pedagogical practices must be continuously examined (1990, pp. 23, 24). By extension, we assert that the purpose of the scholarship of teaching is the development and improvement of pedagogical practices. Classroom research and the development of pedagogical content knowledge offer a conceptually clear basis for the development and improvement of pedagogical practices. Cross (1990) defines classroom research as "any systematic inquiry designed and conducted for the purpose of increasing insight and understanding of the relationship between teaching and learning" (p. 136). The aims of classroom research resonate well with the objective of developing and improving pedagogical practices. *Pedagogical content knowledge* refers to knowledge of the pedagogy specific to an academic discipline, focusing particularly on how to make the subject matter understandable to students (Shulman, 1986). The goal of the scholarship of teaching should be the development and improvement of pedagogical content knowledge. Professorial behaviors reflecting engagement in classroom research and the development of pedagogical content knowledge are exhibited in Appendix B.

The goal of the scholarship of teaching should be the development and improvement of pedagogical practices.

Opportunities for research collaboration with business and industry should be encouraged to foster the scholarship of application. As described in "Factors Affecting the Institutionalization of a Broader Definition of Scholarship," the use of higher education as an instrument of state level economic development and research collaboration between industry and higher education institutions provides faculty in certain academic disciplines—engineering, computer science, medicine, agriculture, chemistry, and biotechnology—with opportunities to engage in the scholarship of application. Such opportunities foster structural level institutionalization of the scholarship of application. Such opportunities exist more commonly for faculty in research and doctoral-granting universities than in comprehensive universities and colleges (Hines, 1988; Fairweather, 1988). Consequently, we recommend that presidents, chief academic officers, academic deans, department chairs, and individual faculty members of applicable departments develop opportunities with local and state businesses and industries for faculty engagement in the scholarship of application.

Procedural Level

Institutional support mechanisms must be developed for faculty scholarship engagement. Faculty workloads present a significant obstacle to procedural level institutionalization of Boyer's call to expand the boundaries of scholarship in liberal arts colleges and comprehensive universities and colleges. Although permanent reductions in teaching loads are not financially feasible in most such institutions, policies can be developed that are designed to assist faculty members in the production of unpublished scholarly outcomes that meet the criteria for scholarship and writing for publication. Temporary reductions in teaching course loads, mini-sabbaticals, release time during the academic year, and summer salary support can give faculty in liberal arts colleges and comprehensive universities and colleges the time needed for engagement in scholarship. Such policies should pertain to faculty members engaged in the domain of scholarship emphasized by their type of college or university: the scholarship of integration and application for comprehensive university and college faculty members and the scholarship of integration and teaching for academics in liberal arts colleges.

In some colleges and universities, a few faculty members are pursuing their doctoral degrees. Faculty members engaged in dissertation research for their doctoral degrees should also receive such support if the topic of their dissertation coincides with the objectives of the scholarship domain stressed by their college or university.

Creativity contracts should become part of institutional policy. Our study confirms the work of Finkelstein (1984) that publication productivity decreases with age, given that faculty professional age negatively influences publication productivity associated with the scholarships of discovery and application. To counter burnout and to provide a renewed sense of purpose for senior faculty members, we recommend that colleges and universities of all types embrace the concept of and adopt creativity contracts as introduced by Boyer (1990). These creativity contracts are essential to faculty renewal and should allow faculty members to flourish even as they reach the latter stages of their careers. For these creativity contracts to be successful, faculty members must be given the freedom to shift their scholarly focus and define professional goals for a three- to five-year period. The recognition of the changing seasons of an academic life will allow faculty to remain energized and therefore more productive. In fact, the scholarships of integration and application likely stand the most to gain as experienced faculty members focus their time and energy on solving consequential problems or exploring other fields. These creativity contracts must be tailored for each senior faculty member to build on individual strengths and sustain productivity across a lifetime.

Publicly observable unpublished scholarship should be used in posttenure reviews. Since the 1980s, posttenure review has been part of the public policy debate (Licata, 1986). To appraise engagement in scholarship, posttenure assessment procedures should include publicly observable but unpublished scholarship and publications associated with the scholarships of application, discovery, integration, and teaching. This recommendation is consistent with Licata's guidelines (1986) that posttenure reviews should include multiple sources of information. Boyer's prescriptions for institutional domain emphasis should also receive consideration in the posttenure review process. For example, do faculty members undergoing posttenure review in liberal arts colleges demonstrate some engagement in the scholarships of integration and teaching? The assessment of teaching effectiveness and service in posttenure reviews should also include the type of scholarly activities focused on service and teaching listed in the inventory of scholarship.

Incorporation Level

Institutional mission statements should emphasize the domain of scholarship stressed by the institution. In the last chapter, we reviewed various approaches to altering the academic reward system and its concomitant scholarship assessment processes and recommended that colleges and universities committed to incorporation level institutionalization of Boyer's arguments use these reviewed approaches as a basis for institutional action. The boards of trustees of colleges and universities taking such actions should endorse these institutional actions. We particularly urge the development of institutional missions following Boyer's prescriptions for the domain of scholarship for emphasis by faculty members in a given type of college or university. In turn, academic reward systems and the process of scholarship assessment must align with the promulgated scholarly objectives stated in the institutional mission. For example, Boyer (1990) asserts that liberal arts college faculty should stress the scholarship of integration and teaching. Thus, the scholarly mission of liberal arts colleges should be the pursuit of scholarship focused on integration and teaching.

We add to the thrust of these suggestions by recommending that the domain or domains of scholarship embraced in an institutional mission statement receive continuous reinforcement by college and university presidents, chief academic officers, academic deans, and department chairs. Messages and signals from such individuals should stress the importance of the institution's scholarship mission. Public speeches, speeches before university assemblies, memoranda, and day-to-day conversations should accentuate, when appropriate, the type or types of scholarship the institution emphasizes. This recommendation resonates with the formulations of cultural leadership. Cultural leadership pertains to the role of leaders in making meaning for organizational members around issues important to the organization (Bensimon, Neuman, and Birnbaum, 1989). In the first recommendation, we advance suggestions for changing the scholarship assessment process.

Tenure and promotion decisions should be based on performance of the type of scholarship stressed by an institution's mission statement. The type of scholarship underscored by an institution's mission statement should provide the basis for decisions about the award of tenure and promotion made by departmental and institutional tenure and promotion committees. We also recommend that college or university tenure and promotion committees acknowledge that faculty members in different academic disciplines vary in their level of engagement in the domains of scholarship. Such differences should be recognized and weighed in decisions about tenure and promotion. This recommendation stems from our findings pertaining to disciplinary differences in domain performance summarized in this chapter. This recommendation also coincides with Diamond's view (1993) that academic reward systems should recognize and acknowledge disciplinary differences.

Graduate school training should foster scholarship in each of Boyer's four domains. Graduate school training is the first, critical step of entry into the professoriate. Scholarly instruction is therefore very important to the development of future faculty members and their perceptions about what scholarly endeavors are worthy of pursuing as faculty members. Successful incorporation level institutionalization of the scholarships of application, integration, and teaching depends largely on alterations in the graduate school training process.

To embrace Boyer's four domains of scholarship (1990), graduate students should be exposed during graduate study to scholarship in the four domains. In particular, the scholarships of teaching, application, and integration need to be incorporated into the ethos of graduate school training. Boyer (1990) reinforces the idea of encouraging graduate students to work across several areas by taking courses in disciplines outside their major. He applies this idea to the dissertation by asserting that faculty from related fields or outside the university be considered as readers on dissertation committees. This practice would bring new insight and expand the overall experience of students, essentially realizing the integration of scholarship for graduate students.

The most problematic area for graduate students is the scholarship of teaching. If a student is assigned to a teaching assistantship, he or she often enters the classroom with no systematic training or guidance. Boyer (1990) suggests that all graduate students participate in a seminar on teaching. Fortunately, an increasing number of universities are creating programs and offering experience to prepare students for college teaching (Gaff and Lambert, 1996). We encourage doctoral-granting institutions that have not developed such programs to do so. We also assert that universities that have such programs should expand them to include not only teaching assistants but also other graduate students who aspire to be college and university professors.

Teaching centers, which have grown in number over the past decade, would be likely candidates for overseeing this education. In addition, academic departments should require a seminar on college teaching for individuals who seek faculty appointments. The foundation for such pedagogical training should be the acquisition of a knowledge base about methods and approaches to college teaching. Such a knowledge base would provide the foundation for the scholarship of teaching. Without such a knowledge base, faculty engagement in the scholarship of teaching becomes tenuous.

The scholarship of integration could also be fostered by seminars that bring together graduate students from different academic departments. Through such seminars, graduate students would have access to peers on their campuses, allowing possible opportunities to expand into the domain of scholarly integration. With peer interactions as a major source of graduate student socialization, contact through the teaching center can enhance the positive aspects of teaching that may not be reinforced in the student's department or discipline.

Ronkowski (1993) discusses socialization through the phases proposed by Sprague and Nyquist (1989): senior learners, colleagues in training, and junior colleagues. Senior learners are new to doctoral training and lack expert knowledge on the subject matter and the university system. Graduate students develop a sense of professional identity and become more assured of their professional skills during the colleagues-in-training stage. Finally, during the junior colleagues stage, doctoral students view themselves more in terms of colleagues with faculty and define themselves as members of this status group.

Each stage offers opportunities to expose graduate students to the four domains of scholarship. As senior learners, students should interact with other graduate students and be encouraged to explore the areas of teaching and discovery. As colleagues in training, they internalize and refine their teaching and discovery skills. This time is appropriate for the scholarship of application as they see the connection between thought and action. Boyer suggests a practicum to foster this development. Last, as junior colleagues, increased exposure through professional organizations, the dissertation defense process, and even the search for a faculty position can reinforce the four domains and importance of being a well-rounded scholar.

In addition, faculty of doctoral programs should support doctoral dissertations focusing on topics pursuing the underlying objectives of each domain of scholarship. Support for such dissertations leads to rectification of the problem with graduate education Richlin (1993) identifies.

Scholarship by community college faculty should be encouraged. Although our study did not include faculty from two-year colleges, other studies document the lack of scholarship produced by faculty members from these institutions (Palmer, 1992). With roughly 41 percent of all colleges and universities two-year institutions, it seems reasonable to include a recommendation for stimulating scholarship by community college faculty members. Therefore, scholarship, not just research, should be elevated at community colleges. More specifically, community college faculty members should internalize the role of scholar to facilitate all three levels of institutionalization of scholarship in general and the scholarship of teaching in particular. Community college faculty members' emphasis on the scholarship of teaching resonates with Boyer's perspective that community college faculty should stress the scholarship of teaching.

Scholarship, not just research, should be elevated at community colleges.

So often, faculty and administrators at two-year colleges proudly proclaim to work at teaching institutions. The debate quickly turns into a zero-sum game in which teaching and research are at odds with one another. Vaughan (1988) accurately points out that the debate for academics at community colleges should be as teacher and scholar versus as teacher only. It is the scholarly passion for learning that sustains effective teaching. Outstanding teaching at a community college or a research I university can occur only through bringing new knowledge and inspiration to the classroom. Only when the vital relationship between teaching effectiveness and scholarship in all of its various forms is recognized, rewarded, and revered by community college presidents, tenure and review committees, and community college faculty will two-year colleges achieve their full potential. Basically, community colleges must develop a culture supporting faculty scholarship in general and the scholarship of teaching in particular.

We advance these recommendations for consideration by presidents, chief academic officers, academic deans, department chairs, faculty tenure and promotion committees, and individual faculty members of colleges and universities. The effectiveness of these recommendations also depends, in part, on the actions of scholarly or disciplinary associations. Many academic fields have adopted statements on the academic reward structure. Because our recommendations focus on implementation by individual colleges and universities, we do not review the various efforts of disciplinary associations. For such statements by academic disciplines, see *The Disciplines Speak: Rewarding the Scholarly, Professional, and Creative Work of Faculty* (Diamond and Adam, 1995, 2000).

Recommendations for Further Study

This section offers seven recommendations for further research.

Three subrecommendations for further study stem from limitations of our study reported in this volume.

- The sample for our study includes five categories of the Carnegie Classification of Institutions. Different results might obtain if all categories of this classification scheme were included. The need to replicate our study in community colleges is particularly pressing. We offer only limited indices of community college faculty engagement in Boyer's four domains of scholarship. The three levels of institutionalization of Boyer's formulations in community colleges can be more completely assessed through such a study.
- The four disciplines represented in our study are classified as pure academic disciplines, according to Biglan's classification (1973) of academic subject matter areas. Thus, our study should be extended to such high

consensus applied academic disciplines as agriculture and engineering and to such low consensus applied fields as economics, finance, and education (Biglan, 1973). Such extensions might result in additional disciplinary differences in faculty engagement in Boyer's domains of scholarship in general and the scholarship of application in particular.

- As previously indicated, our measures of unpublished scholarly outcomes serve as proxy indicators of unpublished publicly observable scholarship. If our measures are put in a form along the lines of our first recommendation, then these scholarly outcomes would fit the criteria of scholarship delineated by Shulman and Hutchings (1998). Accordingly, the survey instrument used in our faculty professional performance study needs refinement. Our measures of unpublished scholarly outcomes, exhibited in Appendix B, should be revised so that these scholarly outcomes are in a publicly observable form. For example, a talk on a disciplinary topic on a local radio station (an integration-oriented unpublished scholarly outcome) should be stated as an audio- or videotape-recorded talk on a current disciplinary topic on a local radio station.

The inventory of scholarship is not exhaustive. Further delineation of scholarly activities, unpublished scholarly outcomes (unpublished publicly observable scholarship), and publications is needed across the four domains of scholarship. Particular attention must be focused on the delineation of various scholarly activities, unpublished scholarly outcomes (unpublished publicly observable scholarship), and publications associated with the visual and performing arts. Such delineation also requires the careful consideration of the relevance of each of Boyer's four domains of scholarship to academic work in the visual and performing arts.

Faculty engagement in the scholarship of teaching in the form of publications and unpublished scholarly outcomes (unpublished publicly observable scholarship) raises a question: What is the relationship between faculty engagement in the scholarship of teaching and effective teaching? Such a question is complex. At one level, we might expect that the scholarship of teaching enhances teaching role performance as knowledge on the development and improvement of pedagogical practice emerges from such scholarship. The teaching role performance of individual faculty members may improve if they read publications or receive unpublished scholarship that appears in an exchangeable form that reports the results of engagement in the scholarship of teaching. The teaching performance of faculty engaged in the scholarship of teaching might also benefit from their own scholarship. Thus, we recommend research that focuses on whether the outcomes of the scholarship of teaching—unpublished scholarly outcomes and publications—enhance teaching effectiveness.

For individuals, we might expect various contrasting relationships: conflict, complementarity, and the null (Braxton, 1996). The conflict perspective would predict a negative relationship between teaching effectiveness and the scholarship of teaching, as time devoted to engagement from the scholarship of teaching may detract from time devoted to teaching role performance. Alternately, the two roles may complement one another, or there may be no relationship between teaching effectiveness and engagement in the scholarship of teaching by individual faculty members.

Braxton and Berger (1996) conclude from various research studies that, with few exceptions, faculty research activity does not negatively affect faculty teaching role performance. Indicators of faculty engagement in the scholarship of teaching were not included in the studies reviewed by Braxton and Berger, however. Consequently, we recommend that the relationship between teaching effectiveness and faculty engagement in the scholarship of teaching at the level of the individual faculty member be the focus of future research.

We concluded that the scholarships of discovery and teaching have achieved structural and procedural level institutionalization. Our study, with the refinements described in the first recommendation for further study, should be conducted again in five to ten years to assess whether efforts to attain structural and procedural level institutionalization of the scholarships of application and integration prove successful. Moreover, such a study is needed to appraise whether incorporation level institutionalization has occurred for any of the domains of scholarship apart from discovery.

Successful attainment of the institutionalization of Boyer's perspectives hinges on implementation of the recommendations we advance in this chapter as well as recommendations posited elsewhere in this volume. Consequently, we recommend studies at colleges and universities implementing one or more recommendations. Such studies should identify problematic and effective aspects of the implementation of the focal recommendation. The findings of such studies would guide the development of efficacious recommendations.

Many colleges and universities indicate consideration of a wider range of procedures to assess teaching, research, and applied scholarship (Glassick, Huber, and Maeroff, 1997). Moreover, reports of institutional efforts to implement Boyer's recommendations for the assessment of scholarship are frequently presented at annual meetings of the Faculty Roles and Rewards Conference sponsored by the American Association for Higher Education. We did not review such reports in this volume. Consequently, these reports—as well as other institutional documents—should be assessed to identify the strengths and weaknesses of different efforts to alter the academic reward structure through assessment procedures at individual colleges and universities. The identification of exemplary institutional practices should be a major objective of such research.

Future studies of publication productivity should distinguish among the four domains of scholarship. Use of general measures of publication productivity masks variations across the four domains, resulting in inaccurate estimates of the level of faculty publication productivity.

Closing Thoughts

Possible solutions to important societal problems, improvement of undergraduate education, the realignment of the faculty reward structure with institutional missions, and the recognition of many day-to-day professional activities constitute likely outcomes of structural, procedural, and incorporation level institutionalization of the scholarships of application, integration, and teaching. In addition, an effective social system of scholarship obtains—a social system that satisfactorily performs the four functions of this social action system: pattern maintenance, adaptation, goal attainment, and integration (Paulsen and Feldman, 1995). An academic reward system that allocates recognition to different ways of knowing represented among college and university faculty also results: abstract-reflective, concrete-reflective, abstract-active, and concrete-active (Rice, 1992). Boyer asserts that the "richness of faculty talent should be celebrated, not restricted" (1990, p. 27). Allocation of recognition among these different ways of knowing ensures such a celebration of talent. Beyond these important outcomes, advancements in knowledge and understanding of the human condition may result from structural, procedural, and incorporation level institutionalization of the scholarships of application, integration, and teaching.

The value of these possible outcomes of structural, procedural, and incorporation level institutionalization of the scholarships of application, integration, and teaching warrants a dedicated effort by presidents, chief academic officers, academic deans, faculty tenure and promotion committees, department chairs, individual faculty members, and scholars of higher education to hasten the full institutionalization of these three domains of scholarship.

Appendix A: Faculty Professional Performance Study

THIS APPENDIX DESCRIBES the methodology and statistical procedures used in our faculty professional performance study, incorporating all statistical tables referred to in the volume.

Methodology

Our study's sampling design and research design are described in this section.

Sample

Full-time college and university faculty members holding tenured, tenure-track, or non-tenure-track academic appointments at five types of colleges and universities and four academic disciplines—biology, chemistry, history, and sociology—constitute the population of inference for this study. The five types of colleges and universities represent categories of the Carnegie Classification of Institutions. A sample of 4,000 faculty members was randomly selected from this population; 200 individuals from each of the four academic disciplines were selected from each of the five types of colleges and universities.

The faculty professional performance survey was mailed to this sample in spring 1999. This survey included professorial behaviors reflecting each of the four domains of scholarship. These behaviors were developed using the work of Boyer (1990), Braxton and Toombs (1982), and Pellino, Blackburn, and Boberg (1984) as a foundation. This survey also contained items measuring characteristics of the faculty such as gender, full- or part-time status, name of university awarding the doctorate, race/ethnicity, tenure status, and year of receipt of doctoral degree. Two experts on faculty scholarly performance established face validity for the various forms of scholarship contained in this survey.

After an initial mailing and two additional mailings to nonrespondents, a total of 1,424 faculty members returned a completed survey instrument, a 35.6 percent rate of response. We conducted t tests and chi-square analyses comparing initial respondents to the survey with individuals who responded to subsequent mailings on the nine dependent and seven independent variables of this study. This method of ascertaining sample bias is consistent with the formulations of Goode and Hatt (1952) and Leslie (1972). These tests indicated that the obtained sample tends to be representative of the population of inference on eight of the nine dependent variables and on six of the seven independent variables. More specifically, the obtained samples demonstrated a slight bias toward faculty with higher levels of discovery-oriented scholarship, as faculty who responded to the initial mailing evidenced slightly higher levels of such productivity ($x = 1.43$) than did faculty members who responded to subsequent mailings ($x = 1.38$). Although statistically reliable, this difference is slight and has little or no influence on the findings pertinent to the scholarship of discovery. The obtained sample is also overrepresented by Caucasian faculty members and underrepresented by Asian academics.

Research Design

The research design for this study comprised nine dependent variables and seven independent variables. The nine dependent variables measured faculty engagement in the four domains of scholarship discerned by Boyer (1990).

Scholarship of Application. Three dependent variables measured faculty engagement in the scholarship of application: scholarly activities oriented toward the scholarship of application, unpublished publicly observable scholarship reflecting the scholarship of application, and publications reporting the outcomes of engagement in the scholarship of application.

Scholarship of Discovery. Faculty engagement in the scholarship of discovery was assessed through one dependent variable: publications oriented toward the scholarship of discovery.

Scholarship of Integration. Two dependent variables appraised faculty engagement in the scholarship of integration: publications reflecting the scholarship of integration, and unpublished publicly observable scholarship manifesting engagement in the scholarship of integration.

Scholarship of Teaching. Scholarly activities oriented toward teaching, unpublished publicly observable scholarship reflecting the scholarship of teaching, and publications emanating from engagement in the scholarship of teaching constituted the three dependent variables measuring faculty engagement in the scholarship of teaching.

These nine dependent variables are composites. Each composite variable was computed by summing individual responses to each type of professorial behavior and then dividing this sum by the total number of types of professorial behaviors subsumed under each dependent variable. Each professorial behavior is contained as a survey item in the faculty professional performance survey. Faculty members responded to the statement "indicate how often you have published any of the following within the past three years" for each specific professorial behavior. The following five-point scale was used to respond: 1 = none, 2 = 1–2, 3 = 3–5, 4 = 6–10, and 5 = 11+. The specific professional behaviors for each dependent variable are exhibited in Appendix B.

Independent Variables

As previously stated, seven independent variables were included in the research design for this study: institutional types, academic discipline, and five faculty characteristics (gender, race/ethnicity, tenure status, prestige of doctoral program, and professional age). Each independent variable was developed using items included in the faculty professional performance survey.

Institutional Type. The five categories of colleges and universities of the Carnegie Classification of Institutions provided the basis for the construction of the independent variable *institutional type:* research universities–I, doctoral-granting universities–I, comprehensive universities and colleges–I, baccalaureate liberal arts colleges–I, and baccalaureate liberal arts colleges–II. These types of institutions vary in terms of their institutional missions. At one extreme, liberal arts colleges–II are predominately oriented toward teaching. At the other extreme, research universities–I and doctoral-granting universities–I are primarily oriented toward research. Comprehensive universities and colleges–I and liberal arts colleges–I hold the middle ground, as their missions tend to be oriented toward both teaching and research (McGee, 1971; Finnegan, 1993).

Academic Discipline. The four academic disciplines included in this study were biology, chemistry, history, and sociology. These four disciplines may be classified as high and low consensus (Biglan, 1973; Lodahl and Gordon, 1972). Biology and chemistry are high consensus disciplines, whereas history and sociology are low consensus disciplines.

Gender. For the variable *gender,* female respondents were coded as *1,* male respondents as *2.*

Race/Ethnicity. Race/ethnicity consisted of three dichotomous variables: white Caucasian (1 = white Caucasian, 0 = other); African American (1 = African American, 0 = other), and Asian (1 = Asian, 0 = other).

Tenure Status. Tenured faculty were coded as *1,* untenured faculty as a *0.*

Prestige of Doctoral Program. The scholarly quality of program faculty ratings developed by the National Research Council's assessment of doctoral programs in 1995 was used to measure the prestige of the doctoral program. The scale ranged from 0 to 5, with *0* denoting that faculty quality was not sufficient for doctoral education. We used the survey item *degree-granting institution* to identify respondents' graduate programs in the National Research Council's assessment of doctoral education. The rating for the scholarly quality of the program faculty was then assigned to this variable.

Professional Age. This variable was constructed using the year the highest earned degree was received. This year was subtracted from 1999 to compute the variable professional age.

Additional Measures: Self- and Social Knowledge

Composite variables measuring self-knowledge and social knowledge regarding each domain of scholarship were developed. Self-knowledge focused on the values espoused by individual faculty members, whereas social knowledge pertained to values espoused by academic departments and the college or university of academic appointment (Blackburn and Lawrence, 1995). For each domain of scholarship, a composite variable was developed to measure the value individual faculty members, departmental colleagues, and the college or university of appointment placed on the focal scholarship. A total of twelve composite measures was developed. Each composite variable was calculated using an item or items included in the faculty professional performance survey. The specific item or items on each scale are exhibited in Table A.6.

Statistical Procedures

This section addresses the statistical procedures used to address the research questions posed in the introduction to this volume. The five research questions serve as an organizing framework.

1. *Do faculty levels of engagement in Boyer's four domains of scholarship resemble the general level of publication productivity found in research?* Percentage distributions across the five categories of the response scale used to measure the nine dependent variables were employed to address this research question. Percentage distributions for each of the nine dependent variables were computed. Table A.1 displays the statistics addressing this question.

2. *Do faculty levels of engagement in Boyer's four domains of scholarship match Boyer's prescriptions for institutional domain emphasis?* For comparisons between institutional types, we used one factor analyses of variance. Institutional type served as the factor, which involved five levels. Nine one-factor analyses of variance were conducted, one for each dependent variable. The Scheffe method of post hoc mean comparisons was used following statistically significant main effects to discern statistically significant group differences. Because the homogeneity of variances assumption

TABLE A.1

Frequency of General Engagement in the Four Domains of Scholarship

Frequency of Performance	Application			Discovery	Integration		Teaching		
	Scholarly Activities	Unpublished Scholarly Outcomes	Publications	Publications	Unpublished Scholarly Outcomes	Publications	Scholarly Activities	Unpublished Scholarly Outcomes	Publications
1.00	4.5%	25.5%	57.1%	27.6%	34.7%	25.9%	0.1%	0.6%	74.7%
1.01 to 1.99	71.4%	68.6%	33.1%	59.3%	59.8%	73.1%	15.4%	32.9%	23.9%
2.00 to 2.99	22.2%	5.4%	7.9%	11.8%	4.9%	1.1%	56.0%	50.1%	1.2%
3.00 to 3.99	1.9%	0.3%	1.2%	1.2%	0.4%	0.2%	25.8%	14.8%	0.3%
4.00 to 4.99	0.3%	0.0%	0.6%	0.1%	0.4%	0.0%	2.7%	1.6%	0.0%
5.00	0.0	0.0%	0.0%	0.0%	0.0%	0.0%	0.0%	0.0%	0.0%
Mean	1.69	1.31	1.29	1.42	1.27	1.18	2.61	2.30	1.09
Standard deviation	0.49	0.35	0.51	0.45	0.41	0.24	0.64	0.67	0.24

Note: Frequency of performance during the previous three years measured using the following response scale: 1 = none, 2 = 1 or 2, 3 = 3–5, 4 = 6–10, and 5 = 11 or greater.

was violated for each of the nine dependent variables, the .01 level of statistical significance was used to reduce the probability of committing Type I errors. Table A.2 exhibits the statistics concentrating on this question.

Dependent t tests were used to make within–institutional type comparisons between the four domains of scholarship. For each institutional type, dependent t tests were performed making comparisons between dependent variables of the same form of scholarship. For example, dependent t tests comparing the performance of scholarly activities associated with application to the performance of scholarly activities associated with teaching were conducted only for liberal arts colleges–II. Table A.3 shows the statistics relevant to this question.

3. *Does faculty publication productivity in Boyer's four domains of scholarship found across different types of colleges and universities mirror the level of general publication productivity exhibited across different types of colleges and universities?* The findings of the nine one-factor analyses of variance executed to address the between–institutional type comparison facet of the above research question also provided the basis for addressing this research question.

4. *Do faculty levels of engagement in Boyer's four domains of scholarship vary across different academic disciplines?* One-factor analyses of variance were performed to address this research question. Academic discipline served as the factor composed of four levels, one for each discipline. Nine one-factor analyses of variance were conducted, one for each dependent variable. The Scheffe method of post hoc mean comparisons was used following statistically significant main effects to discern statistically significant group differences. Because the homogeneity of variances assumption was violated for each of the nine dependent variables, the .01 level of statistical significance was used to reduce the probability of committing Type I errors. Table A.4 displays supporting statistics.

5. *Do individual faculty characteristics influence faculty engagement in the four domains of scholarship? Do individual faculty characteristics influence faculty engagement in the four domains of scholarship in the same way that they influence general publication productivity?* Hierarchical linear multiple regression was the statistical procedure used to address both parts of this

TABLE A.2

Between–Institutional Type Comparisons: Analysis of Variance of Faculty Engagement in the Four Domains of Scholarship by Institutional Type

Domain/Form of Engagement	F-Ratio	Means by Institutional Type					Post Hoc Mean Comparisons
		RU-I	DOC-I	CUC-I	LA-I	LA-II	
Application							
Scholarly activities	11.67**	1.57	1.66	1.77	1.59	1.79	CUC-I greater than RU-I and LA-I*, LA-II greater than RU-I and LA-I*
Unpublished scholarly outcomes	1.01	1.31	1.28	1.32	1.28	1.32	No statistically significant differences
Publications	37.39**	1.56	1.41	1.21	1.18	1.13	RU-I and DOC-I greater than CUC-I, LA-I, and LA-II*
Discovery							
Publications	106.89**	1.78	1.61	1.29	1.32	1.17	RU-I greater than DOC-I, CUC-I, LA-I, and LA-II* DOC-I greater than CUC-I, LA-I, and LA-II*

Integration							
Unpublished scholarly outcomes	0.81	1.24	1.25	1.29	1.27	1.28	No statistically significant differences
Publications	28.39**	1.29	1.24	1.14	1.15	1.12	RU-I and DOC-I greater than CUC-I, LA-I, and LA-II*
Teaching							
Scholarly activities	2.82	2.69	2.63	2.52	2.64	2.58	No statistically significant differences
Unpublished scholarly outcomes	7.20**	2.15	2.21	2.31	2.39	2.39	LA-I and LA-II greater than RU-I*
Publications	0.58	1.10	1.11	1.07	1.09	1.09	No statistically significant differences

Note: RU-I = research universities-I, DOC-I = doctoral-granting universities-I, CUC-I = comprehensive universities and colleges-I, LA-I = liberal arts colleges-I, LA-II = liberal arts colleges-II.

Results of Scheffe method of post hoc mean comparisons following a statistically significant overall F-Ratio.

*p < .01.

**p < .001.

TABLE A.3
Within-Institutional Type Comparisons: *t* Test Comparisons of Means of Faculty Engagement in the Four Domains of Scholarship

Focal Institutional Type	Application			Discovery	Integration		Teaching		
	Scholarly Activities	Unpublished Scholarly Outcomes	Publications	Publications	Unpublished Scholarly Outcomes	Publications	Scholarly Activities	Unpublished Scholarly Outcomes	Publications
Research universities–I	1.57	1.31	1.56	1.78	1.24	1.29	2.69	2.15	1.10
Doctoral-granting universities	1.66	1.28	1.41	1.61	1.25	1.24	2.63	2.21	1.10
Comprehensive universities and colleges–I	1.77	1.32	1.21*	1.29	1.29	1.14*	2.52	2.31	1.07
Liberal arts–I	1.59	1.28	1.18*	1.32	1.26	1.15*	2.64	2.39	1.09**
Liberal arts–II	1.79	1.32	1.13*	1.17	1.28	1.12*	2.58	2.39	1.09**

Note: All mean differences except those marked by an asterisk are statistically significant at p < .01.

*Mean differences are not statistically significant at p < .01.

**Mean difference between integration and teaching publications not statistically significant.

TABLE A.4

Comparisons Among Academic Disciplines: Analysis of Variance of Faculty Engagement in the Four Domains of Scholarship by Academic Discipline

Domain/Form of Engagement	F-Ratio	Means by Academic Discipline				Post Hoc Mean Comparisons
		Biology	Chemistry	History	Sociology	
Application						
Scholarly activities	1.40	1.66	1.67	1.69	1.73	No statistically significant differences
Unpublished scholarly outcomes	14.52**	1.32	1.25	1.24	1.39	Sociology greater than chemistry and history*
Publications	13.07**	1.24	1.40	1.18	1.32	Chemistry greater than biology and history*
Discovery						
Publications	0.75	1.38	1.43	1.41	1.42	No statistically significant differences
Integration						
Unpublished scholarly outcomes	23.85**	1.23	1.15	1.38	1.28	History greater than biology and chemistry.* Sociology greater than biology and chemistry*

(Continued)

TABLE A.4

Comparisons Among Academic Disciplines: Analysis of Variance of Faculty Engagement in the Four Domains of Scholarship by Academic Discipline (Continued)

Domain/Form of Engagement	F-Ratio	Means by Academic Discipline				Post Hoc Mean Comparisons
		Biology	Chemistry	History	Sociology	
Publications	63.08**	1.11	1.12	1.30	1.21	History greater than biology, chemistry, and sociology.* Sociology greater than biology and chemistry*
Teaching						
Scholarly activities	46.90**	2.54	2.32	2.84	2.73	History and sociology greater than biology and chemistry*
Unpublished scholarly outcomes	2.52	2.25	2.25	2.34	2.36	No statistically significant differences
Publications	3.65	1.07	1.11	1.08	1.11	No statistically significant differences

Note: Final column shows results of Scheffe method of post hoc mean comparisons.

* = $p < .01$.

** = $p < .001$.

question. Nine regression equations were estimated, one for each dependent variable. Each dependent variable was regressed on institutional type, academic discipline, and the five faculty characteristics (gender, race/ethnicity, tenure status, prestige of doctoral program, and professional age). The variables were entered in this order. Institutional type was measured using four dichotomous variables representing research universities–I, doctoral-granting universities–I, comprehensive universities and colleges–I, and liberal arts colleges–I. Academic discipline was measured with three dichotomous variables representing the disciplines of biology, chemistry, and history. No multicolinearity problems were identified for any of the nine regressions executed. The results of the regression analyses conducted are exhibited in Table A.5.

In addition, the value placed on each of the four domains of scholarship by individual faculty members, department colleagues, and the college or university of academic appointment was assessed by combining the response categories to the specific item or specific items of each composite variable measuring these values. Two categories of responses were developed from the four-point rating scale used by respondents (1 = strongly disagree, 2 = disagree, 3 = agree, and 4 = strongly agree): strongly agree/agree, and strongly disagree/disagree. The percentage of respondents for each category was computed; the percentages are displayed in Table A.7.

Limitations of the Study

Several limitations of this study temper the conclusions we advance in the last chapter of this volume.

1. The sample obtained for this piece of research was limited to five categories of the Carnegie Classification of Institutions. The use of the full Carnegie Classification system might produce a different pattern of findings. For example, the inclusion of two-year colleges might have resulted in a different configuration of findings regarding the institutionalization of the scholarship of teaching.

TABLE A.5

Influence of Faculty Characteristics: Regression of Faculty Engagement in the Four Domains of Scholarship on Institutional Type, Academic Discipline, and Five Faculty Characteristics

Independent Variables	Application			Discovery	Integration		Teaching		
	Scholarly Activities	Unpublished Scholarly Outcomes	Publications	Publications	Unpublished Scholarly Outcomes	Publications	Scholarly Activities	Unpublished Scholarly Outcomes	Publications
RU-I	-.22*** (.18)	-.01 (-.02)	.25*** (.32)	.56*** (.49)	-.01 (-.02)	.11*** (.26)	.12 (.07)	-.22** (-.13)	-.02 (-.04)
DOC-I	-.09** (-.07)	-.01 (-.02)	.21*** (.27)	.46*** (.39)	.01 (.01)	.09*** (.20)	.10 (.06)	-.10 (-.06)	.00# (.00)
CUC-I	-.03 (-.03)	.00# (.00)	.06 (.09)	.13*** (.12)	-.00# (-.01)	.02 (.05)	-.07 (-.04)	-.09 (-.05)	-.02 (-.05)
LA-I	-.15 (-.14)	-.00# (-.01)	.05 (.08)	.12*** (.12)	.01 (.03)	.03 (.09)	.07 (.04)	.00# (.00)	.00# (.01)
Biology	.01 (.01)	.05 (.09)	.05 (.07)	.00# (.00)	-.08*** (-.17)	-.14*** (-.39)	-.23*** (-.16)	-.09 (-.06)	-.00# (-.00)
Chemistry	.02 (.01)	.00# (.01)	.15*** (.21)	.04 (.03)	-.16*** (-.30)	-.14*** (-.36)	-.46*** (-.31)	-.07 (-.04)	.03 (.09)
Sociology	.05 (.04)	.10* (.19)	.10*** (.15)	.03 (.03)	-.07** (-.13)	-.07*** (-.17)	-.08 (-.05)	-.04 (-.02)	.03 (.08)

Gender	−.01	.00#	.05*	.11***	.03	.03**	−.08	−.23***	−.03
	(−.01)	(.00)	(.08)	(.12)	(.07)	(.08)	(−.08)	(−.16)	(−.09)
White	−.05	−.08	−.04	−.02	−.06	−.02	−.16	−.09	−.01
	(−.03)	(−.11)	(−.04)	(−.01)	(−.08)	(.04)	(−.08)	(−.04)	(−.03)
African American	.29	−.01	.01	−.02	.15*	.04	−.18	−.27	−.02
	(.10)	(−.01)	(.01)	(−.01)	(.11)	(.03)	(−.05)	(−.07)	(−.02)
Asian	.07	−.11	−.03	.05	−.03	.02	−.11	−.04	.02
	(.03)	(−.08)	(−.02)	(.02)	(−.03)	(.02)	(−.03)	(−.01)	(.02)
Program prestige	−.05*	−.02	−.00#	.04*	−.02	.00#	.02	.03	−.00#
	(−.09)	(−.07)	(−.01)	(.09)	(−.07)	(.03)	(.03)	(.04)	(−.01)
Tenure	.11	.01	−.01	.08*	.02	.03	−.02	−.01	.02
	(.10)	(.02)	(−.01)	(.07)	(.04)	(.07)	(−.01)	(−.01)	(.06)
Professional age	.00#	−.04	−.00*	−.01*	.00#	−.00#	−.02***	−.02***	.00#
	(.06)	(−.04)	(−.10)	(−.15)	(.03)	(−.06)	(−.26)	(−.24)	(.01)
Constant	1.80	.34	1.64	0.89	.28	.14	3.29	3.10	3.10
R Squared	.08***	.06***	.14***	.26***	.10***	.21***	.19***	.14***	.11	.05

Note: RU-I = research universities–I, DOC-I = doctoral-granting universities–I, CUC-I = comprehensive universities and colleges–I, LA-I = liberal arts colleges–I, LA-II = liberal arts colleges–II.

Standardized regression coefficients are in parentheses.

= regression coefficient .001 or lower.

* = p < .01.

** = p < .001.

*** = p < .0001.

TABLE A.6
Measurement of the Value Placed on the Four Domains of Scholarship by Individual Faculty, Departmental Colleagues, and the Institution

Value Toward Scholarship	Measurement of the Value Toward Scholarship
Value Placed on the Scholarship of Application	
Individual	This composite measure comprises three survey items: "I believe practical problems frequently require disciplinary knowledge and skill for their solution." "I value knowledge that is obtained from the application of disciplinary knowledge and skill to practical problems." "I value scholarship that applies the knowledge and skill of my academic discipline to practical problems." Cronbach alpha = .87.
Departmental colleagues	This composite measure comprises two survey items: "Most of my departmental colleagues value scholarship that applies the knowledge and skill of an academic discipline to practical problems." "Most of my departmental colleagues value knowledge that is obtained from the application of disciplinary knowledge and skill to practical problems." Cronbach alpha = .84.
Institution	This composite measure comprises two survey items: "At my institution, scholarship that applies the knowledge and skill of the academic disciplines to practical problems is valued." "At my institution, knowledge that is obtained from the application of disciplinary knowledge and skill to practical problems is valued. Cronbach alpha = .93.
Value Placed on the Scholarship of Discovery	
Individual	This measure comprises one survey item: "I value research that leads to new disciplinary knowledge."

TABLE A.6
(Continued)

Departmental colleagues	This measure comprises one survey item: "Most of my departmental colleagues value research that leads to new disciplinary knowledge."
Institution	This measure comprises one survey item: "At my institution, research that leads to new disciplinary knowledge is valued."

Value Placed on the Scholarship of Integration

Individual	This measure includes three survey items: "I value scholarship that derives meaning from the research findings of other scholars." "I value scholarship that identifies underlying patterns in the research findings of other scholars." "I value scholarship that makes connections across different academic disciplines." Cronbach alpha = .78.
Departmental colleagues	This measure comprises three survey items: "Most of my departmental colleagues value scholarship that makes connections across different academic disciplines." "Most of my departmental colleagues value scholarship that identifies underlying patterns in the research findings of other scholars." "Most of my departmental colleagues value scholarship that derives meaning from the research findings of other scholars." Cronbach alpha = .77.
Institution	This measure comprises three survey items: "At my institution, scholarship that makes connections across different academic disciplines is valued." "At my institution, scholarship that derives meaning from the research findings of other scholars is valued." "At my institution, scholarship that identifies underlying patterns in the research findings of other scholars is valued." Cronbach alpha = .84.

(Continued)

Value Toward Scholarship	Measurement of the Value Toward Scholarship
Value Placed on the Scholarship of Teaching	
Individual	This composite measure consists of two survey items: "I believe that many aspects of college teaching may be defined as scholarship." "I value scholarship that contributes to the improvement of college teaching." Cronbach alpha = .56.
Departmental colleagues	This composite measure comprises two survey items: "Most of my departmental colleagues value scholarship that contributes to the improvement of college teaching." "Most of my colleagues believe that many aspects of college teaching may be defined as scholarship." Cronbach alpha = .73.
Institution	This composite measure consists of two survey items: "At my institution, scholarship that contributes to the improvement of college teaching is valued." "At my institution, it is commonly believed that many aspects of college teaching may be defined as scholarship." Cronbach alpha = .75.

Note: Respondents used the following response categories: 1 = strongly disagree, 2 = disagree, 3 = agree, 4 = strongly agree.

2. The four disciplines represented in this study may be classified as pure academic disciplines, according to Biglan's classification (1973). The extension of the current research to applied academic disciplines might result in disciplinary differences in the institutionalization of the scholarship of application as well as the other three domains.

3. The measures of scholarship performance used in this study are not exhaustive of the types of scholarly activities, unpublished scholarly outcomes, and publications across the four domains of

TABLE A.7
Value Placed on the Four Domains of Scholarship by Individual Faculty, Departmental Colleagues, and the Institution

	RU-I		DOC-I		CUC-I		LA-I		LA-II	
	Strongly Agree/ Agree	Strongly Disagree/ Disagree	Strongly Agree/ Agree	Strongly Disagree/ Disagree	Strongly Agree/ Agree	Strongly Disagree/ Disagree	Strongly Agree/ Agree	Strongly Disagree/ Disagree	Strongly Agree/ Agree	Strongly Disagree/ Disagree
Value Placed on the Scholarship of Application										
Individual	93.7%	6.3%	96.5%	3.5%	94.4%	5.6%	92.1%	7.9%	93.6%	6.4%
Departmental colleagues	56.7%	43.3%	69.1%	30.9%	79.4%	20.6%	72.7%	27.3%	79.2%	20.8%
Institution	79.0%	21.0%	81.2%	18.8%	83.0%	17.0%	80.0%	20.0%	79.6%	20.4%
Value Placed on the Scholarship of Discovery										
Individual	98.8%	1.2%	99.2%	0.8%	98.6%	1.4%	96.8%	3.2%	96.4%	3.6%
Departmental colleagues	96.9%	3.1%	92.3%	7.7%	86.9%	13.1%	94.1%	5.9%	82.3%	17.7%
Institution	96.0%	4.0%	92.7%	7.3%	81.8%	18.2%	90.9%	9.1%	76.8%	23.2%

(Continued)

TABLE A.7
(Continued)

	RU-I		DOC-I		CUC-I		LA-I		LA-II	
	Strongly Agree/ Agree	Strongly Disagree/ Disagree	Strongly Agree/ Agree	Strongly Disagree/ Disagree	Strongly Agree/ Agree	Strongly Disagree/ Disagree	Strongly Agree/ Agree	Strongly Disagree/ Disagree	Strongly Agree/ Agree	Strongly Disagree/ Disagree
Value Placed on the Scholarship of Integration										
Individual	93.4%	6.6%	94.2%	5.8%	95.4%	4.6%	94.5%	5.5%	93.9%	6.1%
Departmental colleagues	63.7%	36.3%	63.0%	37.0%	60.2%	39.8%	70.8%	29.2%	68.6%	31.4%
Institution	74.0%	26.0%	77.3%	22.7%	70.0%	30.0%	79.5%	20.5%	70.7%	29.3%
Value Placed on the Scholarship of Teaching										
Individual	76.3%	23.7%	83.7%	16.3%	87.4%	12.6%	83.2%	16.8%	91.1%	8.9%
Departmental colleagues	30.3%	69.7%	43.8%	56.2%	66.8%	33.2%	62.2%	37.8%	80.7%	19.3%
Institution	38.3%	61.7%	52.8%	47.2%	68.4%	31.6%	64.0%	36.0%	80.6%	19.4%

Note: RU-I = research universities–I, DOC-I = doctoral-granting universities–I, CUC-I = comprehensive universities and colleges–I, LA-I = liberal arts colleges–I, LA-II = liberal arts colleges–II.

scholarship. Nevertheless, the measures used are judged to be face valid by two experts on faculty scholarly role performance. Moreover, they stem from empirical research on the scholarly activities of faculty (Braxton and Toombs, 1982; Pellino, Blackburn, and Boberg, 1984; Sundre, 1992).

4. The fourth limitation pertains to the response rate of 35.6 percent to the faculty professional performance survey. A higher rate of response might have resulted in a different configuration of findings. This limitation is blunted to some extent, however, given that the obtained sample is judged to be representative of the population of inference of this inquiry on the vast majority of variables included in this study's research design. Nevertheless, some bias exists in the obtained sample, particularly bias toward higher discovery-oriented publication productivity, overrepresented by Caucasian faculty and underrepresented by Asian faculty members. The effects of such bias on the configuration of findings reported in this volume are minimal.

5. Unpublished scholarly outcomes serve as proxy measures of unpublished publicly observable scholarship. Unpublished scholarly outcomes function as proxy indicators, as they would be publicly observable if put in a form observable by peers.

Appendix B: The Inventory of Scholarship

THIS INVENTORY groups professorial behaviors by their orientation into one of four domains of scholarship delineated by Boyer. These professorial behaviors also fit one of three categories: scholarly activities, unpublished scholarly outcomes, and publications. A distinction between scholarly activities and scholarship undergirds these categories. Scholarly activities use disciplinary knowledge and skill in their performance, whereas scholarship takes the form of unpublished scholarly outcomes and publications. Unpublished scholarly outcomes fully meet the definition of scholarship if they appear in a publicly observable form. By being publicly observable, unpublished scholarly outcomes meet the three criteria for scholarship delineated by Shulman and Hutchings (1998): it must be public, subject to critical review, and in a form that allows use and exchange by other members of the scholarly community. To be publicly observable, unpublished scholarly outcomes need to be in the form of a paper, a taped (audio or video) presentation, written report, or Web site (Braxton and Del Favero, forthcoming).

The Scholarship of Application
Scholarly Activities

Institutional Service/Academic Citizenship
- Service on a departmental program review committee
- Service on a departmental curriculum committee

- Service on a college-wide curriculum committee
- Self-study conducted for one's department
- Service on a committee engaged in institutional preparation for accreditation review
- Study conducted to help solve a departmental problem
- Study conducted to help formulate departmental policy
- Study conducted to help formulate institutional policy

Service to the Lay Public
- Introduction of some result of scholarship in a consultation
- Provision of expert witness or testimony
- Engagement in consulting off campus

Unpublished Scholarly Outcomes
- Development of an innovative technology
- Seminars conducted for laypersons on current disciplinary topics
- Development of a new process for dealing with a problem of practice
- Study conducted for a local organization
- Study conducted for a local nonacademic professional association
- Study conducted for a local government agency
- Study conducted to help solve a community problem
- Study conducted to help solve a county or state problem

Publications
- An article that outlines a new research problem identified through the application of the knowledge and skill of one's academic discipline to a practical problem
- An article that describes new knowledge obtained through the application of the knowledge and skill of one's academic discipline to a practical problem
- An article that applies new disciplinary knowledge to a practical problem
- An article that proposes an approach to the bridging of theory and practice
- An article reporting findings of research designed to solve a practical problem

The Scholarship of Discovery

Unpublished Scholarly Outcomes

- A paper presented that describes a new theory developed by the author*
- A paper presented that reports the findings of research designed to gain new knowledge*
- A report on research findings to a granting agency*

Publications

This list includes only publications associated with the traditional scholar. Such publications best serve the academic system necessary for the dissemination of outcomes of engagement in the scholarship of discovery (Fox, 1985). For example:

- A book chapter describing a new theory developed by the author
- A refereed journal article reporting findings of research designed to gain new knowledge
- A book reporting findings of research designed to gain new knowledge
- A book describing a new theory developed by the author
- A refereed journal article describing a new theory developed by the author

The Scholarship of Integration

Unpublished Scholarly Outcomes

- A talk on a current disciplinary topic given on a local radio station
- A talk on a current disciplinary topic given on a local television station
- A talk on a current disciplinary topic given for a local men's or women's service organization
- A talk on a current disciplinary topic given for a local business organization
- A talk on a current disciplinary topic given for a local nonacademic professional association
- A talk on a current disciplinary topic given for a group of college alumni

An asterisk (*) designates a professorial behavior *not* included in a composite measure of faculty engagement. See "Research Design" section in Appendix A for a description of these composite measures.

- A lecture on a current disciplinary topic given for a local high school class
- A lecture on a current disciplinary topic given for a high school assembly
- A lecture on a current disciplinary topic given at a local community college

Publications

- A review of literature on a disciplinary topic
- A review of literature on an interdisciplinary topic
- A review essay of two or more books on similar topics
- An article on the application of a research method borrowed from an academic discipline outside one's own
- A book chapter on the application of a research method borrowed from an academic discipline outside one's own
- An article on the application of a theory borrowed from an academic discipline outside one's own
- A book chapter on the application of a theory borrowed from an academic discipline outside one's own
- A critical book review published in an academic or professional journal
- A critical book review published in a newsletter of a professional association
- An article addressing current disciplinary topics published in the popular press
- A book addressing a disciplinary/interdisciplinary topic published by the popular press
- An article that crosses subject matter areas
- A book that crosses subject matter areas
- A critical book review published in the popular press
- A book published reporting research findings to lay readers
- A textbook published
- An edited book published
- An article on a current disciplinary topic published in a local newspaper

- An article on a current disciplinary topic published in a college or university publication
- An article on a current disciplinary topic published in a national magazine of the popular press

The Scholarship of Teaching

Scholarly Activities

- Directed student research projects
- Preparation of a new syllabus for a course
- Development of examination questions requiring higher-order thinking skills
- Development of a set of lectures, learning activities, or class plans for a new course
- Maintenance of a journal of day-to-day teaching activities
- Study problems or questions emerging from one's own teaching
- Construction of an annotated bibliography for course reference
- A lecture on topics from current journal articles not covered in course readings
- A lecture on topics from current scholarly books not covered in course readings
- Development of a new course
- Development of a new set of lectures for an existing course
- Introduction of some result of one's scholarship in teaching

Unpublished Scholarly Outcomes

General Pedagogical Development and Improvement

- Presentation about new instructional techniques to colleagues
- Development of a collection of resource materials for one's subject area
- Construction of a novel examination or testing practice

Classroom Research

- Experimentation with new teaching methods or activities
- Development of methods to make ungraded assessments of students' learning of course content
- Trying a new instructional practice and altering it until it is successful

Pedagogical Content Knowledge
- Development of examples, materials, class exercises, or assignments that help students to learn difficult course concepts
- Creation of an approach or strategy for dealing with class management problems faced in teaching a particular type of course
- Creation of an approach or strategy to help students to think critically about course concepts

Publications

General Pedagogical Development and Improvement
- Publication listing resource materials for a course
- Publication on the use of a new instructional method

Classroom Research
- Publication reporting a new teaching approach developed by the author
- Publication of a method to make ungraded assessments of students' learning of course content
- Publication on the use of a new instructional practice and the alterations made to make it successful

Pedagogical Content Knowledge
- Publication on examples, materials, class exercises, or assignments that help students to learn difficult course concepts
- Publication on an approach or strategy for dealing with class management problems faced in teaching a particular type of course
- Publication on an approach or strategy to help students to think critically about course concepts

References

Baldridge, J. V., Curtis, D. V., Ecker, G., and Riley, G. L. (1978). *Policy making and effective leadership.* San Francisco: Jossey-Bass.

Baldwin, R. G., and Austin, A. E. (1995). Toward greater understanding of faculty research collaboration. *Review of Higher Education, 19*(2), 45–70.

Becher, T. (1989). *Academic tribes and territories: Intellectual inquiry and the culture of disciplines.* Bristol, PA: Open University Press.

Bell, S., and Gordon, J. (1999). Scholarship: The new dimension to equity issues for academic women. *Women's Studies International Forum, 22*(6), 645–658.

Bensimon, E. M., Neuman, A., and Birnbaum, R. (1989). *Making sense of administrative leadership: The "L" word in higher education.* ASHE-ERIC Higher Education Report, No. 1. Washington, D.C.: Graduate School of Education and Human Development, The George Washington University.

Berman, P., and McLaughlin, M. W. (1974). *Federal programs supporting educational change: Vol. 1. A model of educational change.* Santa Monica, CA: Rand Corp.

Biglan, A. (1973). The characteristics of subject matter in different academic areas. *Journal of Applied Psychology, 57*(3), 195–203.

Blackburn, R. T. (1974). The meaning of work in academia. In J. Doi (Ed.), *Assessing faculty efforts.* San Francisco: Jossey-Bass.

Blackburn, R. T., and Lawrence, J. H. (1995). *Faculty at work: Motivation, expectation, satisfaction.* Baltimore: Johns Hopkins University Press.

Blumenthal, D., Epstein, E., and Maxwell, J. (1986). Commercializing university research: Lessons from the experience of the Wisconsin alumni research fund. *New England Journal of Medicine, 314*(25), 1621–1626.

Boyer, E. L. (1990). *Scholarship reconsidered: Priorities of the professoriate.* Princeton, NJ: Carnegie Foundation for the Advancement of Teaching.

Boyer, E. L. (1994a). Creating the new American college. *Chronicle of Higher Education, 40*(27), 48.

Boyer, E. L. (1994b). *Scholarship reconsidered: Priorities for the new century.* London: National Commission on Education and Council for Industry and Higher Education.

Boyer, E. L. (1996). The scholarship of engagement. *Journal of Public Service and Outreach, 1*(1), 11–20.

Braskamp, L. A., and Ory, J. C. (1994). *Assessing faculty work: Enhancing individual and institutional performance.* San Francisco: Jossey-Bass.

Braxton, J. M. (1986). The normative structure of science: Social control in the academic profession. In J. C. Smart (Ed.), *Higher education: Handbook of theory and research: Vol. 2* (pp. 309–357). New York: Agathon Press.

Braxton, J. M. (1993). Deviancy from the norms of science: The effects of anomie and alienation in the academic profession. *Research in Higher Education, 34*(2), 213–228.

Braxton, J. M. (1995). Disciplines with an affinity for the improvement of undergraduate education. In N. Hativa and M. Marincovich (Eds.), *Disciplinary differences in teaching and learning: Implications for practice* (pp. 59–64). San Francisco: Jossey-Bass.

Braxton, J. M. (1996). Contrasting perspectives on the relationship between teaching and research. In J. M. Braxton (Ed.), *Faculty teaching and research: Is there a conflict?* (pp. 5–14). New Directions for Institutional Research, No. 90. San Francisco: Jossey-Bass.

Braxton, J. M., and Bayer, A. E. (1986). Assessing faculty scholarly performance. In J. W. Creswell (Ed.), *Measuring faculty research performance* (pp. 25–42). San Francisco: Jossey-Bass.

Braxton, J. M., and Berger, J. B. (1996). Public trust, research activity, and the ideal of service to students as clients of teaching. In J. M. Braxton (Ed.), *Faculty teaching and research: Is there a conflict?* (pp. 79–91). New Directions for Institutional Research, No. 90. San Francisco: Jossey-Bass.

Braxton, J. M., and Del Favero, M. (Forthcoming). Evaluating scholarship performance: Traditional and emergent assessment templates. In C. Colbeck (Ed.), *Evaluating faculty performance.* New Directions for Institutional Research, No. 114. San Francisco: Jossey-Bass.

Braxton, J. M., and Hargens, L. L. (1996). Variation among academic disciplines: Analytical frameworks and research. In J. C. Smart (Ed.), *Higher education: Handbook of theory and research: Vol. 11* (pp. 1–46). New York: Agathon Press.

Braxton, J. M., Olsen, D., and Simmons, A. (1998). Affinity disciplines and the use of principles of good practice for undergraduate education. *Research in Higher Education, 39,* 299–318.

Braxton, J. M., and Toombs, W. (1982). Faculty uses of doctoral training: Consideration of a technique for the differentiation of scholarly effort from research activity. *Research in Higher Education, 16,* 265–282.

Centra, J. A. (1980). *Determining faculty effectiveness: Assessing teaching, research, and service for personnel decisions and improvement.* San Francisco: Jossey-Bass.

Centra, J. A. (1993). *Reflective faculty evaluation: Enhancing teaching and determining faculty effectiveness.* San Francisco: Jossey-Bass.

Centra, J. A. (2001, February). *A model for assessing the scholarship of teaching.* Paper presented at the 9th Annual AAHE Conference on Faculty Roles and Rewards, Tampa, FL.

Clark, T. N. (1971). Institutionalization of innovations in higher education: Four models. In J. V. Baldridge (Ed.), *Academic governance: Research on institutional politics and decision making* (pp. 75–96). Berkeley, CA: McCutchan.

Cohen, A. M., and Brawer, F. B. (1982). *The American community college.* San Francisco: Jossey-Bass.

Cole, J. R., and Cole, S. (1973). *Social stratification in science.* Chicago: University of Chicago Press.

Creamer, E. G. (1998). *Assessing faculty publication productivity: Issues of equity.* ASHE-ERIC Higher Education Report, Vol. 26, No. 2. Washington, D.C.: Graduate School of Education and Human Development, The George Washington University.

Creswell, J. W. (1985). *Faculty research performance: Lessons from the sciences and social sciences.* ASHE-ERIC Higher Education Report, No. 4. Washington, D.C.: Association for the Study of Higher Education.

Cross, K. P. (1990). Classroom research: Helping professors learn more about teaching and learning. In P. Seldin and Associates (Eds.), *How administrators can improve teaching: From talk to action in higher education.* San Francisco: Jossey-Bass.

Cross, K. P. (1998). Classroom research: Implementing the scholarship of teaching. In T. Angelo (Ed.), *Classroom assessment and research: An update on uses, approaches, and research findings* (pp. 5–12). New Directions for Teaching and Learning, No. 75. San Francisco: Jossey-Bass.

Cross, K. P., and Steadman, M. H. (1996). *Classroom research: Implementing the scholarship of teaching.* San Francisco: Jossey-Bass.

Curry, B. K. (1991). Institutionalization: The final phase of the organizational change process. *Administrator's Notebook, 35*(1).

Davis, W. E., and Chandler, T.J.L. (1998). Beyond Boyer's *Scholarship Reconsidered*: Fundamental changes in the university and the socioeconomic systems. *Journal of Higher Education, 69*(1), 23–64.

Deal, T. E., and Kennedy, A. E. (1982). *Corporate cultures: The rites and rituals of corporate life.* Reading, MA: Addison-Wesley.

Diamond, R. M. (1993). Changing priorities and the faculty reward system. In R. M. Diamond and B. E. Adam (Eds.), *Recognizing faculty work: Reward systems for the year 2000* (pp. 5–12). New Directions for Higher Education, No. 81, San Francisco: Jossey-Bass.

Diamond, R. M. (1999). *Aligning faculty rewards with institutional mission: Statements, policies and guidelines.* Bolton, MA: Anker Publishing.

Diamond, R. M., and Adam, B. E. (Eds). (1995). *The disciplines speak: Rewarding the scholarly, professional, and creative work of faculty: Vol. 1.* Washington, D.C.: American Association for Higher Education.

Diamond, R. M., and Adam, B. E. (Eds). (2000). *The disciplines speak: Rewarding the scholarly, professional, and creative work of faculty: Vol. 2.* Washington, D.C.: American Association for Higher Education.

Driscoll, A., and Lynton, E. A. (1999). *Making outreach visible: A guide to documenting professional service and outreach.* AAHE Forum on Faculty Roles and Rewards. Washington, D.C.: American Association for Higher Education.

Dunn, D. S., and Zaremba, S. B. (1997). Thriving at liberal arts colleges: The more correct academic. *Teaching of Psychology, 24*(1), 8–14.

Edgerton, R., Hutchings, P., and Quinlan, K. (1991). *The teaching portfolio: Capturing the scholarship in teaching.* Washington, D.C.: American Association for Higher Education.

Ewell, P. T. (1994, January). *The neglected art of collective responsibility: Restoring our links with society.* Commissioned paper for the American Association for Higher Education Forum on Faculty Roles and Rewards Second Annual Conference, New Orleans, LA.

Fairweather, J. S. (1988). *Entrepreneurship and higher education.* ASHE-ERIC Higher Education Report, No. 6. Washington, D.C.: Graduate School of Education and Human Development, The George Washington University.

Fairweather, J. S. (1996). *Faculty work and public trust: Restoring the value of teaching and public service in American academic life.* Boston: Allyn & Bacon.

Finkelstein, M. J. (1984). *The American academic profession.* Columbus: Ohio State University Press.

Finnegan, D. E. (1993). Segmentation in the academic labor market: Hiring cohorts in comprehensive universities. *Journal of Higher Education, 64,* 621–656.

Fox, M. F. (1985). Publication, performance, and reward in science and scholarship. In J. C. Smart (Ed.), *Higher education: Handbook of theory and research: Vol. 1* (pp. 255–282). New York: Agathon Press.

Froh, R. C., Gray, P. J., and Lambert, L. M. (1993). Representing faculty work: The professional portfolio. In R. A. Diamond and B. E. Adam (Eds.), *Recognizing faculty work: Reward systems for the year 2000.* San Francisco: Jossey-Bass.

Fulton, O., and Trow, M. (1974). Research activity in American higher education. *Sociology of Education, 47,* 29–73.

Gaff, J. G., and Lambert, L. M. (1996, July/August). Socializing future faculty to the values of undergraduate education. *Change, 28,* 38–45.

Gaston, J. (1971). Secretiveness and competition for priority of discovery in physics. *Minerva, 9,* 472–492.

Glassick, C. E., Huber, M. T., and Maeroff, G. I. (1997). *Scholarship assessed: Evaluation of the professoriate.* San Francisco: Jossey-Bass.

Goode, W. J., and Hatt, P. K. (1952). *Methods of social research.* New York: McGraw-Hill.

Goodman, P. S., and Associates (Eds.). (1982). *Change in organizations.* San Francisco: Jossey-Bass.

Hagstrom, W. O. (1965). *The scientific community.* New York: Basic Books.

Halpern, D. F., and others (1998). Scholarship in psychology: A paradigm for the twenty-first century. *American Psychologist, 53*(12), 1292–1297.

Handlin, O. (1986). Epilogues—Continuities. In B. Baily, D. Fleming, O. Handlin, and S. Thernstrom (Eds.), *Glimpses of Harvard's past* (p. 131). Cambridge, MA: Harvard

University Press; and (1990). . . . In D. Bok, *Universities and the future of America* (p. 105). Durham, NC, and London: Duke University Press.

Hines, E. R. (1988). *Higher education and state governments: Renewed partnerships, cooperation, or competition?* ASHE-ERIC Higher Education Report, No. 5. Washington, D.C.: Graduate School of Education and Human Development, The George Washington University.

Huber, M. T. (1998). *Assessing* Scholarship Assessed: *Case studies of faculty evaluation.* Paper presented at the Boyer Legacy: Prospects for a New Century, Hershey, PA, June 4–6.

Hutchings, P. (1999). Scholarship is the big picture. *Carnegie Chronicle,* 7–10.

Hutchings, P., and Shulman, L. S. (1999). The scholarship of teaching: New elaborations, new developments. *Change, 31*(5), 10–15.

Jacoby, R. (1987). *The last intellectuals: American culture in the age of academe.* New York: Basic Books.

Johnston, R. K. (1998). The university of the future: Boyer revisited. *Higher Education, 36,* 253–272.

Katz, D. A. (1973). Faculty salaries, promotion, and productivity at a large university. *American Economic Review, 63,* 469–477.

Kreber, C. (2001a). Conceptualizing the scholarship of teaching and identifying unresolved issues: The framework for this volume. In C. Kreber (Ed.), *Scholarship Revisited: Identifying and implementing the scholarship of teaching* (pp. 1–18). San Francisco: Jossey-Bass.

Kreber, C. (2001b). The scholarship of teaching and its implementation in faculty development and graduate education. In C. Kreber (Ed.), *Scholarship revisited: Identifying and implementing the scholarship of teaching* (pp. 79–88). San Francisco: Jossey-Bass.

Kuhn, T. S. (1962). *The structure of scientific revolutions.* Chicago: University of Chicago Press.

Ladd, E. C. (1979). The work of American college professors: Some data and an argument. *Current Issues in Higher Education.* Washington, D.C.: American Association for Higher Education.

Leslie, L. L. (1972). Are response rates essential to valid surveys? *Social Science Research, 1,* 323–334.

Levine, A. (1994). Service on campus. *Change, 26*(4), 4–5.

Licata, C. M. (1986). *Post-tenure faculty evaluaion: Threat or opportunity?* ASHE-ERIC Higher Education Report, No. 1. Washington, D.C.: Association for the Study of Higher Education.

Lidstone, J. E., Hacker, P. E., and Oien, F. M. (1996). Where the rubber meets the road: Revising promotion and tenure standards according to Boyer. *Quest, 48,* 200–210.

Light, D. (1974). The structure of the academic profession. *Sociology of Education, 47,* 2–28.

Lodahl, J. B., and Gordon, G. G. (1972). The structure of scientific fields and the functioning of university graduate departments. *American Sociological Review, 37*(1), 57–72.

Logan, L. B., and Stampen, J. O. (1985). Smoke stack meets ivory tower: Collaborations with local industry. *Educational Record, 66*(2), 26–29.

Lynton, E. A. (1983). A crisis of purpose: Reexamining the role of the university. *Change, 15,* 18–23, 53.

Lynton, E. A. (1995). *Making the case for professional service. Forum on faculty roles and rewards.* Washington, D.C.: American Association for Higher Education.

Massy, W. F., and Zemsky, R. (1994). Faculty discretionary time: Departments and the academic ratchet. *Journal of Higher Education, 65*(1), 1–22.

McGee, R. (1971). *Academic Janus.* San Francisco: Jossey-Bass.

Merton, R. K. (1957). Priorities in scientific discovery. *American Sociological Review, 2,* 635–659.

Merton, R. K., Reader, G. G., and Kendall, P. L. (1957). *The student-physician.* Cambridge, MA: Harvard University Press.

Meyer, K. A. (1998). *Faculty workload studies: Perspectives, needs, and future directions.* ASHE-ERIC Higher Education Report, vol. 26, No. 1. Washington, D.C.: Graduate School of Education and Human Development, The George Washington University.

Milem, J. F., Berger, J. B., and Dey, E. L. (2000). Faculty time allocation: A study of change over twenty years. *Journal of Higher Education, 71*(4), 454–475.

Miller, R. I. (1972). *Evaluating faculty performance.* San Francisco: Jossey-Bass.

Miller, R. I. (1987). *Evaluating faculty for tenure and promotion.* San Francisco: Jossey-Bass.

Mullins, N. C. (1973). *Science: Some sociological perspectives.* Indianpolis: Bobbs-Merrill.

Nelson, R. (1986). Institutions supporting technical advance in industry. *American Economic Review, 76*(2), 186–190.

Palmer, J. C. (1992). The scholarly activities of community college faculty: Results of a national survey. In J. C. Palmer and G. B. Vaughan (Eds.), *Fostering a climate of faculty scholarship at community colleges* (pp. 49–65). Washington, D.C.: American Association of Community and Junior Colleges.

Park, S. M. (1996). Research, teaching and service: Why shouldn't women's work count? *Journal of Higher Education, 67*(1), 46–80.

Parsons, T., and Platt, G. M. (1973). *The American university.* Cambridge: Harvard University Press.

Parsons, T., and Smelser, N. J. (1956). *Economy and society.* New York: Free Press.

Paulsen, M. B. (2001). The relation between research and the scholarship of teaching. In C. Kreber (Ed.), *Scholarship revisited: Identifying and implementing the scholarship of teaching* (pp. 19–29). San Francisco: Jossey-Bass.

Paulsen, M. B., and Feldman, K. A. (1995). Toward a reconceptualization of scholarship: A human action system with functional imperatives. *Journal of Higher Education, 66*(6), 615–640.

Pellino, G. R., Blackburn, R. T., and Boberg, A. L. (1984). The dimensions of academic scholarship: Faculty and administrator views. *Research in Higher Education, 20,* 103–115.

Peters, L., and Fusfeld, H. (1983). Current U.S. university/industry research connections. In *University-industry research relationships: Selected studies.* Washington, D.C.: National Science Foundation.

Polanyi, M. (1967). *The tacit dimension.* Garden City, NY: Doubleday.

Ramaley, J. A. (2000). Embracing civic responsibility. *AAHE Bulletin, 52*(7), 9–13.

Rice, R. E. (1991). The new American scholar: Scholarship and the purposes of the university. *Metropolitan Universities: An International Forum, 1*(4), 7–18.

Rice, R. E. (1992). Toward a broader conception of scholarship: The American context. In T. G. Whiston and R. L. Geiger (Eds.), *Research universities: The United Kingdom and the United States* (pp. 117–129). Buckingham, Eng.: SRHE and the Open University.

Rice, R. E. (1998, June 5). *Scholarship reconsidered.* Paper presented at the Boyer Legacy: Prospects for a New Century, Hershey, PA.

Richlin, L. (1993). Graduate education and the U.S. faculty. In L. Richlin (Ed.), *Preparing faculty for the new conceptions of scholarship.* New Directions for Institutional Research, No. 54. San Francisco: Jossey-Bass.

Richlin, L. (2001). Scholarly teaching and the scholarship of teaching. In C. Kreber (Ed.), *Scholarship revisited: Identifying and implementing the scholarship of teaching.* San Francisco: Jossey-Bass.

Rokeach, M. (1973). *The nature of human values.* New York: Free Press.

Ronkowski, S. A. (1993). Scholarly teaching: Developmental stages of pedagogical scholarship. In L. Richlin (Ed.), *Preparing faculty for the new conceptions of scholarship* (pp. 79–90). New Directions for Teaching and Learning, No. 54. San Francisco: Jossey-Bass.

Ruscio, K. P. (1987). The distinct scholarship of the selective liberal arts college. *Journal of Higher Education, 58,* 205–221.

Schön, D. A. (1995, November/December). Knowing-in-action: The new scholarship requires a new epistemology. *Change,* 27–35.

Seldin, P. (1980). *Successful faculty evaluation programs: A practical guide to improve faculty performance and promotion/tenure decisions.* Crugers, NY: Coventry Press.

Seldin, P. (1991). *The teaching portfolio: A practical guide to improved performance and promotion/tenure decisions.* Boston: Anker Publishing.

Shulman, L. S. (1986). Those who understand: Knowledge growth in teaching. *Educational Researcher, 15,* 4–14.

Shulman, L. S. (1987). Knowledge and teaching: Foundation of the new reform. *Harvard Educational Review, 57*(1), 1–22.

Shulman, L. S., and Hutchings, P. (1998). *About the scholarship of teaching and learning: The Pew scholars national fellowship program.* Menlo Park, CA: The Carnegie Foundation for the Advancement of Teaching.

Slaughter, S., and Leslie, L. L. (1997). *Academic capitalism: Politics, policies and the entrepreneurial university.* Baltimore: Johns Hopkins University Press.

Slaughter, S., and Silva, E. T. (1985). Towards a political economy of retrenchment: The American public. *Review of Higher Education, 8*(4), 295–318.

Sprague, J., and Nyquist, J. D. (1989). TA supervision. In J. D. Nyquist, R. D. Abbott, and D. H. Wulff (Eds.), *Teaching Assistant Training in the 1990s.* New Directions for Institutional Research, No. 39. San Francisco: Jossey-Bass.

Sundre, D. L. (1992). The specification of the content domain of faculty scholarship. *Research in Higher Education, 33*(3), 297–315.

Toombs, W. (1977). Awareness and use of "academic research." *Research in Higher Education, 7,* 743–765.

Tucker, M. (1986). State economic development and education: A framework for policy development. In *Living on the leading edge.* Lexington, KY: Council of State Governments.

Tuckman, H. P. (1976). *Publication, teaching and the academic reward system.* Lexington, MA: Lexington Books.

Tuckman, H. P., and Hagemann, R. P. (1976). An analysis of the reward structure in two disciplines. *Journal of Higher Education, 47,* 447–464.

Van Doren, M. (1959). *Liberal education.* Boston: Beacon Press.

Vaughan, G. B. (1988). Scholarship in community colleges: The path to respect. *Educational Record 69*(2), 26–31.

Volkwein, F. J., and Carbone, D. A. (1994). The impact of departmental research and teaching climates on undergraduate growth and satisfaction. *Journal of Higher Education, 65,* 147–167.

Wofsy, L. (1986). Biotechnology and the university. *Journal of Higher Education, 57*(5), 477–492.

Zlotkowski, E. (1996). A new voice at the table? Linking service-learning and the academy. *Change, 28*(1), 20–27.

Zlotkowski, E. (1997). Millennial expectations: Creating a new service agenda in higher education. *Quest, 49,* 355–368.

Zuckerman, H. E. (1977). Deviant behavior and social control in science. In E. Sagarin (Ed.), *Deviance and social change* (pp. 87–138). Beverly Hills, CA: Sage.

Zumeta, W. (1987). *Increasing higher education's contribution to economic development in urban and rural communities: Lessons from Washington state.* Paper presented at the Annual Meeting of the Association for the Study of Higher Education, Baltimore, MD.

Name Index

Olsen, D., 4
Ory, J. C., 19

P

Palmer, J. C., 80, 112
Park, S. M., 47
Parsons, T., 20, 32, 40, 65
Paulsen, M. B., 19, 20, 21, 32, 33, 40, 49, 58, 60, 65, 116
Pellino, G. R., 15, 16, 17, 18, 25, 32, 94, 119, 139
Peters, L., 73
Platt, G. M., 20, 32, 40, 65
Polanyi, M., 47

Q

Quinlan, K., 58, 59

R

Ramaley, J. A., 30
Reader, G. G., 78
Rice, R. E., 1, 12, 19, 21, 22, 27, 45, 46, 47, 57, 58, 60, 65, 117
Richlin, L., 24, 62, 63, 78, 79, 90, 112
Riley, G. L., 88
Rokeach, M., 81
Ronkowski, S. A., 57, 58, 111
Ruscio, K. P., 3, 47, 50

S

Schön, D. A., 22, 23, 95
Seldin, P., 15, 58

Shulman, L. S., iii, v, vi, 1, 25, 26, 58, 60, 61, 62, 90, 94, 105, 114, 141
Simmons, A., 4
Slaughter, S., 73
Smelser, N. J., 20
Sprague, J., 111
Stampen, J. O., 74
Steadman, M. H., 60
Sundre, D. L., 25, 94, 139

T

Toombs, W., 15, 16, 17, 18, 25, 32, 78, 94, 119, 139
Trow, M., 3, 36, 42, 99
Tucker, M., 72
Tuckman, H. P., 77

V

Van Doren, M., 46
Vaughan, G. B., 80, 81, 112
Volkwein, F. J., 11

W

Wofsy, L., 73

Z

Zaremba, S. B., 48
Zemsky, R., 75
Zlotkowski, E., 30, 31, 48
Zuckerman, H. E., 78
Zumeta, W., 72

Subject Index

ASHE-ERIC
Higher Education Reports

The mission of the Educational Resources Information Center (ERIC) system is to improve American education by increasing and facilitating the use of educational research and information on practice in the activities of learning, teaching, educational decision making, and research, wherever and whenever these activities take place.

Since 1983, the ASHE-ERIC Higher Education Report series has been published in cooperation with the Association for the Study of Higher Education (ASHE). Starting in 2000, the series has been published by Jossey-Bass in conjunction with the ERIC Clearinghouse on Higher Education.

Each monograph is the definitive analysis of a tough higher education problem, based on thorough research of pertinent literature and institutional experiences. Topics are identified by a national survey. Noted practitioners and scholars are then commissioned to write the reports, with experts providing critical reviews of each manuscript before publication.

Six monographs in the series are published each year and are available on individual and subscription bases. To order, use the order form at the back of this issue.

Qualified persons interested in writing a monograph for the series are invited to submit a proposal to the National Advisory Board. As the preeminent literature review and issue analysis series in higher education, the Higher Education Reports are guaranteed wide dissemination and provide national exposure for accepted candidates. Execution of a monograph requires at least a minimal familiarity with the ERIC database, including *Resources in Education* and the current *Index to Journals in Education*. The objective of these reports is to bridge conventional wisdom and practical research.

A Broader View of Scholarship Through Boyer's Four Domains

Advisory Board

Susan Frost
Office of Institutional Planning
and Research
Emory University

Kenneth Feldman
SUNY at Stony Brook

Anna Ortiz
Michigan State University

James Fairweather
Michigan State University

Lori White
Stanford University

Esther E. Gottlieb
West Virginia University

Carol Colbeck
Pennsylvania State University

Jeni Hart
University of Arizona

Consulting Editors
and Review Panelists

Ann Austin
Michigan State University

John Centra
Syracuse University

Carol Colbeck
Pennsylvania State University

Dorothy E. Finnegan
College of William and Mary

Deborah Hirsch
University of Massachusetts

Mark Oromaner
Hudson County Community
College

Eugene Rice
American Association for Higher
Education

Jack Schuster
Claremont Graduate University

Recent Titles

Volume 29 ASHE-ERIC Higher Education Reports

1. Facilitating Students' Collaborative Writing
   Bruce W. Speck

Volume 28 ASHE-ERIC Higher Education Reports

1. The Changing Nature of the Academic Deanship
   Mimi Wolverton, Walter H. Gmelch, Joni Montez, and Charles T. Nies

2. Faculty Compensation Systems: Impact on the Quality of Higher Education
   Terry P. Sutton, Peter J. Bergerson

3. Socialization of Graduate and Professional Students in Higher Education:
   A Perilous Passage?
   John C. Weidman, Darla J. Twale, Elizabeth Leahy Stein

4. Understanding and Facilitating Organizational Change in the 21st Century: Recent
   Research and Conceptualizations
   Adrianna J. Kezar

5. Cost Containment in Higher Education: Issues and Recommendations
   Walter A. Brown, Cayo Gamber

6. Facilitating Students' Collaborative Writing
   Bruce W. Speck

Volume 27 ASHE-ERIC Higher Education Reports

1. The Art and Science of Classroom Assessment: The Missing Part of Pedagogy
   Susan M. Brookhart

2. Due Process and Higher Education: A Systemic Approach to Fair Decision Making
   Ed Stevens

3. Grading Students' Classroom Writing: Issues and Strategies
   Bruce W. Speck

4. Posttenure Faculty Development: Building a System for Faculty Improvement
   and Appreciation
   Jeffrey W. Alstete

Back Issue/Subscription Order Form

Copy or detach and send to:
Jossey-Bass, 989 Market Street, San Francisco, CA 94103-1741

Call or fax toll free!
Phone 888-378-2537 6AM-5PM PST; Fax 800-605-2665

Individual reports:

Please send me the following reports at $24 each
(Important: please include series initials and issue number, such as AEHE 27:1)

1. AEHE _____

_____

_____

$ _____ Total for individual reports

$ _____ Shipping charges (for individual reports **only;** subscriptions are exempt from shipping charges): Up to $30, add $5^{50} • $30^{01}–$50, add $6^{50} $50^{01}–$75, add $8 • $75^{01}–$100, add $10 • $100^{01}–$150, add $12 Over $150, call for shipping charge

Subscriptions

Please ❏ start my subscription to *ASHE-ERIC Higher Education Reports* at the following rate (6 issues):
U.S.: $130   Canada: $130   All others: $178

$ _____ Total individual reports and subscriptions (Add appropriate sales tax for your state for individual reports. No sales tax on U.S. subscriptions. Canadian residents, add GST for subscriptions and individual reports.)

Federal Tax ID 135593032   GST 89102-8052

❏ Payment enclosed (U.S. check or money order only)

❏ VISA, MC, AmEx, Discover Card # _____ Exp. date _____

Signature _____ Day phone _____

❏ Bill me (U.S. institutional orders only. Purchase order required.)

Purchase order #_____

Name _____

Address _____

_____

Phone_____ E-mail _____

For more information about Jossey-Bass, visit our Web site at:
www.josseybass.com   **PRIORITY CODE = ND1**

John M. Braxton is professor of education and coordinator of the higher education program in the Department of Leadership, Policy, and Organizations at Peabody College, Vanderbilt University. His research interests include the sociology of the academic profession with particular interest in faculty teaching and scholarship role performance and the various social forces that influence such role performances. The social control of faculty research and teaching misconduct is also a major research interest of Professor Braxton.

He has edited two books relevant to his program of research, *Perspectives on Scholarly Misconduct in the Sciences* (1999) and *Faculty Teaching and Research: Is There Conflict?* (1996). He coauthored, with Alan E. Bayer, *Faculty Misconduct in Collegiate Teaching* (1999). Braxton serves as a consulting editor for the *Journal of Higher Education* and *Research in Higher Education.* Professor Braxton is also president-elect of the Association for the Study of Higher Education.

Bill Luckey is the president of Lindsey Wilson College in Columbia, Kentucky. He has served in various administrative positions for the past 19 years. Prior to assuming the presidency, he served as vice president for administration and finance, vice president for development, and vice president for enrollment management. He has an Ed.D. and MBA from Vanderbilt University and earned his BA from Wabash College

Luckey's primary research interests include the roles of faculty members at small private colleges and the scholarship of teaching. His dissertation focused on measuring the faculty engagement in Boyer's four domains of scholarship at Baccalaureate I and II colleges and universities.

Patricia Helland is a doctoral student at Vanderbilt University, where her research has focused primarily on faculty issues and graduate student education. She has authored an article for the *Journal of Student Retention* and has contributed entries to the *Encyclopedia of Higher Education,* the *Encyclopedia of Women in Higher Education,* and the *Encyclopedia of Education.* Helland holds a master's degree from Cumberland University (Human Relations Management). She is pursuing a Ph.D. in higher education administration.